Wanda,
Knowing you has
been and is a joy!
Keep walking your path
with power!

Sherry

Who's Got The Compass?...

I Think I'm Lost!

A Guide to Finding Your Ideal Self

Who's Got The Compass?...

I Think I'm Lost!

A Guide to Finding Your Ideal Self

Sherry Buffington

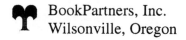
BookPartners, Inc.
Wilsonville, Oregon

BookPartners, Inc.
P.O. Box 922
Wilsonville, Oregon 97070

Dedication

This book is dedicated to some of the most important people in my life. My husband, George, my three children, Gina, Randy and Ron, my grandson, Bryan, and to the memory of my mother, Mary Etta.

They have all shown and taught me unconditional love, joy and acceptance. They have demonstrated faith in me and my abilities, even during the times when I lacked faith in myself. They have been there through thick and thin and have taught me that love is trustworthy and dependable beyond the understanding of pure intellect. They have taught me to live fully, to love completely and to play purposefully. These have been among the finest lessons I could ever hope to gain in life; lessons that have served me well in times past and that continue to serve me daily.

To these six especially, and then to the rest of my wonderful family, all of whom have contributed in unique and loving ways to the experiences that have woven and shaped my life.

This is dedicated, too, to all the other wonderful people I have had the privilege to meet and to know.

To both family and friends I give my heartfelt thanks for all you've added to my life. You have validated to me the truths that are apparent only in the great gifts of unconditional love and acceptance. You've loved me with all my flaws and I love you greatly in return.

This is also dedicated to YOU, the reader, with a world of hope and faith in your ability to find your own path, purpose and passion.

Acknowledgments

I would like to thank my daughter, Gina, for everything she has contributed to the creation of this book. Her contributions have been many and have spanned many years. Specifically, I would like to thank her for her faith in me and her endless assistance in the editing and proofing of the manuscript. She spent many hours reading and re-reading, making corrections and suggestions along the way.

I want to thank my husband George for his encouragement, support and patience. He never complained about the dinners he ended up cooking on many occasions or the evenings spent alone as I sat glued to my computer. And my son Ron for always being there to keep the computer functioning normally and for bailing me out of many computer type nightmares.

I would also like to thank Terry Balser of BookPartners, for her suggested changes which resulted in a far better final product that what I began with; Sheryl Mehary for her excellent work on the text design and for keeping the contents of this book true to my original intent; Richard Ferguson for an outstanding cover design; and Suzanne Deakins for acting as point person to push this project through.

To all of you my heartfelt thanks. I couldn't have done it without you!

Table of Contents

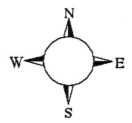

Foreword

I have often wondered how so many of us can reach adulthood with great stores of knowledge in areas such as English, math, geography, job skills, the names of actors, sports figures, song titles, and all kinds of other subjects yet lack important information about the one thing we have owned since we were born — *ourselves.* It seems we spend so much time and energy trying to learn about the world around us, that we neglect learning about the world within. Then we reach adulthood, realize we have somehow lost our way, and begin the search that we hope will eventually lead us to the self we were born to be.

I began my own search when I was twenty-four. Prior to that time I thought lost, frightened, frustrated and insecure was how life was supposed to feel. It took me another ten years to plant my feet firmly on my own personal path, but when I finally found it, my entire life improved dramatically!

Finding my own path was a struggle. It took me much longer than it should have, because I didn't know how or where to look. Not until I was thirty-two, did I finally begin to assemble all the bits and pieces of information I had gathered over the years, and discovered they formed a clear map of the path I should follow. With a map to follow, the way out of a lifelong fog became clear, and by thirty-four I loved the life I was living and the path I found myself on. I still do.

Oh sure, it has its twists and turns, and occasionally obstacles pop up, but I am traveling a path of my own choosing and I wouldn't change a thing! My life has purpose and passion now. Where fear and uncertainty were once the order of the day, I now approach life with confidence and enthusiasm. Rather than viewing daily living as something to just try to struggle through, I see life as a great adventure.

The years I spent searching were not spent in vain. In fact, they turned out to be the wisest investment I ever made. My search led me to the greatest gift I could ever give myself, that of being wholly alive. It has also turned out to be the greatest gift I could have given my family, friends and all the other people in my life. When we have become whole and wholly alive, we can contribute wholly to our own well-being and we can give wholly to others, as well. From this perspective, we know and live happiness and contentment, which we extend quite naturally to others. We begin to love and accept ourselves and this too extends naturally to loving and accepting others. What begins with self eventually extends to our whole world, and that holds true whether or not the attributes we are developing are positive.

When I was unhappy and insecure, I'm sure I extended those conditions to other people too. Most everyone has been victimized by someone intent on projecting their misery onto them, and most have also been privileged to know those who spread joy. Since we can only use and share what we own, we are our own greatest detriment or our own greatest gift, depending on which elements we have chosen to develop. Becoming your own greatest gift requires self-awareness, self-love and self-directedness, and it requires you to find and walk your own path.

This book is about finding your ideal path. In that sense, it is a treasure map. The treasure you will find, when you have worked through all the exercises, gathered all the tools, and taken all the steps, is your finest self. And you can be certain that this self is a real treasure.

This map will guide you from wherever you are now, through the land of self-discovery, and onto your own special lifepath. Once you are on your own path, the rest of the journey will be delightful.

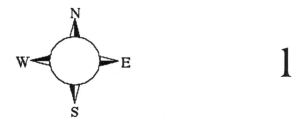

Through the Land of the Lost

"The mass of men lead lives of quiet desperation".
Henry David Thoreau (1817-1862)

Not much has changed since Thoreau penned his now famous words. The majority of people still grope and stumble through life, searching for happiness, love, self-acceptance and contentment. Even in an age when we have the ability to explore the moon and Mars, and answer complex questions about our world and worlds beyond, we still lack the answers to many of our own dilemmas. And we still wander through life, feeling lost, confused and, yes, even desperate.

These pervasive feelings are more than just uncomfortable. They can be downright painful at times. That's why the search for a way to eliminate them occupies so much of our time and energy, and why those who have given up the search seem to move through life numb, as if in a daze. The years of fruitless searching have left them without direction or hope.

Those who continue to search for many years, and down many avenues, often begin to fear that their prospects for happiness and contentment are all but nonexistent. Their lives feel so hopeless and unhappy that they would be willing to exchange them with almost anyone, if that were possible.

That was my position for much of my first thirty years. I had no idea who I was or what I needed to be doing. I felt, and acted, like a lost and frightened child. Having no direction of my own, I followed first this person and then that one. I attached my dreams to whoever appeared to have some idea where they were going. Each in turn became my new guide, and each time I found myself stumbling down the wrong path.

It wasn't the fault of the person I was following, mind you. Most of the time they didn't even know I was following them. I ended up lost and confused, because those I chose to follow were confidently walking their own paths, and their paths were not *mine*. But I had no idea what mine was. I wasn't even aware that there was a path for me. All I knew was there was something wrong with my life. I just couldn't make myself fit into the life I was leading or the box my past had placed me in. I thought I could somehow exchange my unsatisfactory lifestyle for a better one; one like someone else was living.

Exchanging lifestyles — now there's an idea for you. Imagine that you could pick any lifestyle you wanted. Imagine that your choices were limited only by your ability to choose well and to effectively live the lifestyle you had chosen. Right now, at this moment, how prepared would you be to choose your perfect lifestyle? Would you choose days filled with high adventure? If you did, would the constant excitement soon wear you down or would it continue to stimulate you? Or perhaps you would choose a nice, comfortable, predictable, no-worry kind of lifestyle. Would you be content with that forever or would you eventually find it boring and uninteresting? How do you know?

When we don't have a clear vision of ourselves or of the lifestyle that would fit us most perfectly, we try to emulate the lives of others. We let our parents, teachers, bosses, friends, even celebrities or the latest "success" guru dictate our lives for us. When we choose poorly, it's because we don't really know what we need from life. Those who try to guide us usually mean well, but there is no way someone else can give you an accurate picture of who and what it is you are supposed to be. Even if they have walked a similar path, they can't lead you to your own personal ideal, because no one on earth — no one that is, except *you* — can know exactly what you need to live a happy, fulfilling life.

You are completely unique and your ideal path is unique as well. Others may have blazed a similar trail, but there will be places where your uniqueness will require you to leave the path, even if just briefly, and go where no human has gone before you.

Some people don't feel quite prepared to walk an unblazed trail, even well into adulthood. They may feel the way I did, like a toddler stumbling through life, able to maintain a slow, unsteady gait, but still unable to run or skip or dance. Or they may see life as too big to take hold of, like a giant chest filled with wonderful treasures, very desirable, but heavily locked and guarded, always out of reach and impossible to really own.

For some, life is still too fuzzy, too vague, too unclear to bring into focus. They haven't yet managed to find the story line that would allow them to write and direct their own play, so they spend their lives just sitting on the sidelines watching the real life dramas of other people. Or they lose themselves in television, movies, books and other forms of entertainment or distractions. When life feels uncomfortable and uncertain, it can seem safer to just watch, to divert ourselves from the reality of it with various forms of amusement.

Until we have found our own ideal path, the journey through life can seem bewildering, frightening and over-whelming. It can seem like one long, confusing maze that appears to be going somewhere, but which keeps crossing back over itself, and returning right back to the starting point. Except, each time we arrive back at the start we are older, a little more skeptical, and a lot more confused. It seems easier to avoid such confusion than to find ways to live within it, and keeping ourselves distracted seems to be the easiest answer.

But after awhile, distraction isn't enough; it isn't fulfilling; it isn't even distracting anymore. The discomfort has grown to the point that now we have to do something. We can't just watch life happen anymore. We know somehow that if we continue to just watch, we will die a slow, deeply painful emotional death, and we know we will be forced to face this death daily. Upon reaching this point, we must answer the big question: What, exactly, should we *do?*

When we reach adulthood without a clear vision of who we are and where we are going, as many of us do, we must eventually stop, refocus and redirect our lives, if we are ever to know contentment. But, knowing what to focus on and what direction we should take, requires sufficient self-awareness and self-understanding, and to gain that, we must find our way beyond the land of the lost. We must discover our true nature, and understand how our nurturing has altered it for better or for worse. We must explore our values and beliefs, and determine whether they are beneficial or not. We need to inventory our strengths and weaknesses, learn ways to compensate for the weaknesses, and develop the strengths. We need tools for enhancing and optimizing our lives, and for bringing all these elements into focus.

If you are an adult who has not yet defined yourself, your direction and your ideal lifestyle, you are by no means alone. I have met and worked with thousands of lost souls over the years.

Mike is one example of this. He was fifty-four years old when he attended one of my self-discovery workshops. I always ask attendees what they hope to achieve during our time together, and when I asked Mike that question, he replied, "Well, this may sound really strange, since I'm fifty-four years old, but the truth is, I'd like to know what it is I'm supposed to be when I grow up!"

He wasn't laughing when he made that statement, and neither was I. I fully understood. I knew exactly what he meant and I knew it was no joke! It isn't uncommon to hear fully grown and observably intelligent adults make such statements. "I *want* to be happy," they say. "I *want* to do the right thing. I *want* to get my life on track, but I don't know what I should be doing or even where to start."

Like Mike, many people spend most of their lives desperately searching for that one path that will lead them home. Home. Not necessarily to fame and fortune (although some may find those things along the way) but to the peacefulness, contentment and certainty that tells us ... "Yes ... this is it! *This* is where I belong!"

I continued to work with Mike, coaching and counseling him as he made his way to his own ideal path. In less than two years he was a happy, directed man with goals and plans for achieving them. He made a quantum leap toward a happy, contented life by discovering two important things: how to identify and read the road signs that would lead him home, and how to use the compass that nature had provided to keep himself on track.

I keep in touch with many of my clients and students to follow their progress. Watching them transform into happy, self-directed people is a wonder to behold. Sometimes, as in Mike's case, the transformation is very rapid, and for some, it can occur more slowly. But the result of knowing one's self and finally finding one's own ideal path through life is so rewarding that any amount of time and effort spent to that end is a wise and worthwhile investment.

People who are aware of their true selves, and who are living harmonious lives, invariably report higher levels of enthusiasm in their work and personal lives, greater passion for life, and more positive outcomes. They become more directed and more effective at work, in relationships and as a person. And they always *love* their own unique path, once on it. They are setting their own goals and following their own dreams. They know exactly where they belong and they love it!

Those who follow the dreams of others are doomed to lead lives of desperation. A classic example is Princess Diana of Wales. She had everything we might imagine could bring happiness and contentment. She had power, position, money, fame — even a prince for a husband and a castle to live in. But she wasn't happy. She wasn't fulfilled. She was living someone else's dream. The Prince's? The Queen's? England's? Who knows? The only thing we can be really sure of is the dream she was living *wasn't* her own.

Whose dream (or nightmare) have you been living? If your life has been unfulfilling or difficult up to now, you can bet money you haven't been living your dream or walking your own path. You see, your own path is the easiest one to walk, because it's perfectly natural for you, and what's natural is almost effortless. Getting to that point will take some effort, however, so let's get started. It's time to get out the maps and the gear, plan your route, and begin the journey toward your own ideal.

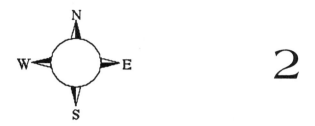

A Time for New Beginnings

"Whistler's mother was in her eighties when she took up painting and discovered she had found her niche!" Vanessa told me. "When I learned that, I decided if she could do it at eighty-something, I could darn sure do it at sixty-something."

Vanessa was a fellow student when I was in college. I admired her courage and her positive outlook. You didn't see many older people attending college back then. In fact, at sixty-seven, I think Vanessa was the oldest student in the school at the time.

I was in my thirties and feeling old, compared to the twenty-year-old students that made up the majority of the student body. "Why, you're just a kid!" Vanessa told me. "You haven't even lived half your life yet! When I started college after my husband died, I was sixty-five, but I figured if I were ever going to fulfill my lifelong dream I'd better get started. Then I thought, 'When would there ever be a better time for me than now?'"

When, indeed. There is never a better time than now and it's really never too late to begin! Life doesn't decree that we must become who we were meant to be in the first twenty years of our lives. Few people have the knowledge or maturity to make lifelong decisions that early, so life gives us lots of chances to get it right.

In truth, we are learning in some way, in every age, and at every time of our lives. Life itself is a great classroom and we are all students, whether we want to be or not. Each day there are new lessons. Some of the lessons are good and some are not so good; some lead to growth; some to stagnation or even decline; some move us toward trust, love and friendship; some toward deceit, ill feelings and loneliness; some lift us up and some knock us down. Some of life's lessons can lead us to our own deliverance, while others might lead us hopelessly astray. Which of life's lessons we focus on and which we choose to keep and use, will surely determine our destiny.

How do we choose wisely? And, if we have chosen poorly in the past, how do we cast away those poor decisions and choose again? And, if we choose again, how can we know what we should choose this time?

Exactly what determines a life well lived? What determines whether we will have a wonderfully inspired, productive, joyous life or a life of misery and despair? If we are lifelong learners, why do so many of us fail to learn something as seemingly simple as how to live our own lives well?

From the day we were born we began gathering knowledge and skills, and putting these together in whatever manner seemed most reasonable to us and most acceptable to all the significant others in our lives at the time (father, mother, siblings, grandparents or other caretakers, friends, teachers). Because acceptance meant survival when we were small children, we worked especially hard at gaining it — so hard, that many of us lost ourselves in the process and by adulthood, the self we were born to be was lost.

In place of the true self, we found, and came to identify with, a mask; the false self that masquerades as the real thing. For some, the mask begins to develop so early in life that the natural self is completely obscured. These people may live an entire lifetime behind the disguise adopted as a child, never even glimpsing their true selves, and never understanding why life is such a struggle.

Ridding ourselves of false beliefs and perceptions can be, and often is, a lot of work. And it's work we must each do for ourselves. No one else can do it for us. Neither can we do it for someone else, no matter how much we love them and want to rescue them. That we can't really change other people is one of life's more difficult lessons. Even those we love very much and would love to help, must ultimately change themselves. We can provide the tools for change, but each individual must pick those tools up and use them.

The first step to claiming or reclaiming our own lives is to eliminate the false beliefs that keep us blind to who we really are. This isn't always easy, but even a glimpse of what lies behind that mask can inspire us to keep working at removing it.

There is only one thing that can absolutely assure your success, at any age, and there is only one thing that can stop you. That one thing is *you.*

Marie was sixty-two when she attended one of my assertiveness workshops, accompanied by her thirty-two year old daughter, Ann. Marie was there, she informed the

class, because she was very passive. She let people, especially her husband, walk all over her. Her life was becoming
ever more miserable and she was seeking a cure. She wasn't
sure what she should do, but she knew something had to
change.

Ann, her daughter, said that she was there because the
assertiveness workshop had altered the life of a friend of
hers in some very positive ways. She could see how
unhappy her mother was, so she brought her, hoping for
similar results.

As Ann was telling the group about the changes in her
friend, and how she hoped her mother might have a similar
result, Marie interjected, "But, your friend is still young! I
may be too old and set in my ways to change now. I've been
this way as long as I can remember." Addressing me, she
asked, "Do you think it's too late for me to change now?"

I gave her the same good and honest advice my
college mate, Vanessa, had given me ten years earlier; it is
never too late, and the only time to begin is now. So, at
sixty-two Marie began exploring new directions.

Like Marie, many adults believe that they are stuck
with whatever attributes they reach adulthood with, and that
as adults, they can change themselves very little, if at all.
Stymied by these beliefs, they reach for and expect little or
no change. Others believe that after adulthood they can only
change the way they *do* things, rather than the way they *are*.
These people go through life trying to fix things outside
themselves and try as they may, they continue to find themselves right back in the same miserable place, with the same
old problems.

Considering that most adults have completed their
formal learning by the age of twenty-five, it's understand-
able that many believe that whatever we are when we reach

adulthood is what we are stuck with. Fortunately, that is not true. Humans are capable of learning and growing, both formally and informally, as long as the brain is functioning properly. For most of us, that means we can learn throughout life.

I learned most of what I know and use in my life today as an adult, and I have witnessed many other adults do the same. Marie made great strides with the help and encouragement of her daughter, and emerged an amazingly strong woman. Her husband, at sixty-eight, was relieved to see her becoming strong and independent enough to take care of herself. He was pleased, he told her, to know he would not have to worry about her should something happen to him. She told me that her only regret was that she hadn't started sooner.

Marie's childhood was similar to mine in that she had an aggressive father and a passive mother. Like me, she had chosen to model her passive mother because the aggression of her father looked too scary. I understood, because I had been where Marie was on every count. I knew her concerns and her feelings of helplessness. I knew how lost, alone, frightened and insecure she felt at times.

I understood how easy it was to leave a dysfunctional home and go right into a dysfunctional marriage. It's extremely common for people to marry a replica of the parent they felt least loved by. It doesn't have to be the parent of the opposite sex. It can be either parent. But whenever we marry a copy of a difficult parent, we set ourselves up to continue living with the pain we lived with as a child. I did that myself when I was eighteen years old.

My childhood was very strictly controlled, and I was kept mostly isolated from the outside world. My father was a rigid disciplinarian, who never trusted people. He was convinced that anyone outside the family would either hurt us or lead us astray, so "outsiders" were kept away.

I grew up, shy, frightened and lacking in social skills and, because I had no idea how to relate to anyone outside my family, I continued to avoid people long after leaving that environment. I remained guarded. I kept my feelings, my wants, my needs to myself. I continued to live with the fear and distrust I had learned as a child. And, true to the pattern, I married a man who was, in his own way, just as strict and unyielding as my father had been.

For six years I remained in the marriage that simulated my childhood experience. I was kept just as isolated, over-controlled and under-nurtured as I had been as a child. I was just as frightened and insecure, too. But, at twenty-four, my nature began to assert itself and urged me to grow up.

I tried to grow up within the marriage, but my husband was accustomed to the child he had married, and any signs of maturity were extremely unsettling to him. In time, I realized I could never mature in this environment, and my need to grow up began to overpower my insecurities.

It is commonly believed that we make changes in our life only as a result of some event that causes us to back up and reevaluate. That is true *only* when it comes to changing our *belief systems*. Changing the direction of our lives often comes as a result of many years of discomfort or psychological pain. In such cases, there is really no particular *event* we can pinpoint as the determining factor. We only know we've reached the point where we are no longer willing to accept the path we are on.

That's exactly what happened with me, and although I had married right out of high school, and had no job skills, no social skills, no training and no sense of direction, I knew I had to get away. I had absolutely no idea where I would go, what I would do or how I would do it. All I knew was that I had to do something! So, with nothing but my clothes and a prayer, I stepped out of the confines of my past and into a world of unknowns.

I felt even more frightened, insecure and lost at first. I had given up or lost everything that was familiar and dear to me, and to say it was tough is a real understatement. I had nothing to fall back on financially, emotionally, professionally, socially or experientially. Just one thing was certain: from my starting point, I had nowhere to go but up.

My first job was working as a waitress. I didn't mind the work, but interacting with people was really hard for me. My old programs and belief systems were still working perfectly, so I was certain people should be avoided, and that was hard to do as a waitress.

The anxiety I felt from the daily contact with "strangers," still gnawed at me, even after eight months as a waitress, so I decided I needed to find a "safer," more comfortable, line of work. I began searching for a profession that would allow me the isolation I had grown accustomed to as a child, and settled on bookkeeping and accounting (all numbers and few people).

I enrolled in a business college and managed to land a job keeping books for an air-conditioning company six months before I graduated. I thought I had finally arrived! Little did I know, I wasn't even in the right neighborhood yet, much less on the right road. I stayed with the accounting profession for eight years, but every year was harder than the one before.

By the sixth year I was again looking for a different profession. This time, I had no idea what was wrong. I was making good money. I didn't have to deal with people directly. I had weekends free. What on earth was the problem now? If *this* wasn't what I should be doing, what was?

At that time, I was the administrative manager for a large recreational vehicle dealership, and I wrote everyone's paychecks. The salespeople in that organization were making the most money. They also seemed to be having the most fun. If I could just learn to be comfortable around people, I thought, maybe I could learn to sell.

I decided I should go back to college and take some marketing classes, thinking they would teach me the skills I needed to become a salesperson. It took only about three days for the professor to inform the class that marketing and selling are two totally different functions. And I realized, to my dismay, that the marketing courses were not what I needed. What I didn't know was that they would lead me, indirectly, to the profession that would become my passion and to the field of study that would finally set me on the right path.

Like many people in our work-ethic culture, I defined myself back then by the work I did. I had no other markers to go by. When the work failed to make me happy, I simply looked for something else, some other work, to which I could attach my identity.

Along the way, I tried photography, interior design, landscape design, selling, and an assortment of other professions, but none of them hit the mark. I stayed with selling the longest and eventually became quite good at it, but not until I stopped defining myself by the work I did and began to take a whole new approach.

After four months of failure as a salesperson, a co-worker who was a really good salesman, told me that the secret to success in selling, and almost everything else, was in fully understanding people, including *yourself.* He suggested that I stop worrying about selling techniques and start learning about what really counted in any transaction — the *people* involved. I was determined to do whatever it took, so I began the study of human nature, starting with myself. That's when things got really interesting.

It was the late seventies, the era of self-improvement, and I hopped right on the self-improvement train. I tried just about every self-improvement plan I could find. I spent days, weeks and years studying philosophy, psychology, world religions and various personal growth plans. I studied the gurus of business, the gurus of sales, the gurus of religion and the gurus of life — anything I thought might help me.

The marketing courses I had taken earlier had given me a taste of psychology during the study of why people buy or don't buy, and why certain messages affect people, while others don't. I found it fascinating that people could be that predictable. I wanted to know more — more about other people and more about myself. But, my interest went far beyond the desire to improve my selling abilities. I soon discovered I loved this field of study.

At the time, I was still very shy and afraid of people, but something inside me begged to be more sociable. Part of me wanted to hide and part of me wanted to be right in the middle of everything, which was completely confusing. So, what did I do? I signed up for some more psychology courses. The more I studied, the more I knew that I had finally found my niche, at least professionally. I didn't understand why at the time, I just knew it felt right. I could fully identify with people who were lost, confused, and hurting emotionally and psychologically.

Because the first eight years out on my own had been spent searching, studying, learning, striving, hoping, trying, failing, and trying again, without any evidence of real progress, I had convinced myself that I had some serious and irreparable flaw, which I wasn't sure psychology, or anything else, could eliminate.

My worst failures came from early attempts at becoming more sociable, and all the psychology and other self-help devices I studied seemed useless in this area. I was simply too afraid of people and no amount of knowledge or self-coaxing seemed to help. I was doing much better relating to people in the selling arena, but the social scene was a whole different story!

Emerson said, "Do the thing you fear and the fear will disappear." It took me several years to really learn that crucial truth. I knew the words — I knew the principle behind the words, but until I moved them to actual experience, I remained stuck.

I was an observer of life back then. I watched other people living their lives and hoped that, by watching, I would somehow evolve in the right direction. I lived life vicariously, watching the socially accomplished meet and mingle. I marveled at the way their conversations flowed. They smiled, they laughed, they played, they made small talk. Occasionally, they would get into serious, intellectual conversations and would practically glow and sparkle with the energy they generated among themselves.

For me any form of social contact, especially carrying on a conversation, was a gut-wrenching experience that I both loathed and longed for. I usually kept to myself though, retreating to the safety of daydreams where I could envision myself surrounded by adoring crowds, with whom I imagined myself laughing, talking easily, entertaining and impressing.

In my daydreams, I became one of those personable, charismatic people I so envied. And from the sidelines, I managed to convince myself that I was making progress, until someone in real life would approach me and speak. Then reality would come crashing in, leaving me stammering, embarrassed and searching for the right thing to say. That's all it would take to send me crawling back into isolation for a long time. As badly as I wanted to make friends and find a perfect mate someday, something inside me, which I could neither grasp nor eliminate, kept me at a "safe" distance from everyone, except family members, who had always been my safe haven.

Those huge walls I had built to protect myself from strangers so many years before had become my personal prison, within which I managed to maintain and somehow justify, my friendless existence.

My main goals at that time revolved around trying to learn how to develop relationships and how to become *very* successful. Unfortunately, I took the idea of success way too far. The books on "success" often suggested that "success in life" meant being a millionaire, complete with the big house, big cars, yachts, and lots of power. I bought into the image and decided I too wanted all the trappings, and I wanted them now.

I kept reading that you had to set goals, develop plans, use positive affirmations, follow your dreams, work hard, waste no time, not get sidetracked by relationships or leisure pursuits and stay focused. Do all this, the gurus promised, and someday you'll be rich! Some self-help books implied that my results would be fast, fabulous and forever, if I followed *the plan*. So, I kept setting goals, making plans, working harder and harder, and telling myself how great I would soon be doing. I kept dreaming and scheming, and I kept falling short — very short, and I had no idea why. I seemed to sabotage myself at every turn.

The harder I tried, the worse things got and the more miserable I became!

After several years of disappointment and despair, I finally discovered what was at the root of all my problems. It was that darn mask! The one that told me I was shy, passive, afraid of people, insecure, incapable of being strong and independent, flawed and undeserving of success. The false image had completely clouded my vision and prevented me from seeing other possibilities.

An amazing thing occurs when your vision finally begins to clear. All those bits and pieces of information you have gathered over the years, all those things you tried to do, all those seemingly failed efforts, somehow begin fitting together and making sense. You realize that your authentic self has kept all the necessary bits and pieces of information and discarded the rest. It has been busily assembling these into clearly readable road signs, and once you can finally read those signs, they all seem to be pointing, miraculously, toward a path that is yours, and yours alone. All the seemingly purposeless seeking somehow comes together and you discover it all had some value after all. What you thought was a waste of time and effort turns out to be pieces to a map that will eventually lead you to your treasure.

No learning is ever really wasted. It all eventually flows together into one great pool, like streams to rivers, and rivers to the sea. Some of what we learn teaches us what we *don't* want from life and some of it teaches us what we must have to be happy and whole. All these lessons help to create the crucial personal boundaries that we begin to use to identify ourselves and the path we should be walking.

It is never too late for a new beginning. We can begin at any time, but we can not begin in any place. We must always begin *within* ourselves, and with our *real* selves.

The false self will invariably hold us back and keep us off track.

The first goal then is to find your authentic self and discover what that self needs to feel happy, content and complete. But, for your authentic self to fully emerge, you'll need to chip away some of the old ideas and beliefs you've adopted and get beneath the disguise; to do that, you'll need some tools.

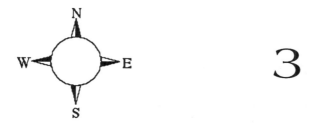

Packing the Right Gear

When my daughter, Gina, was fifteen months old, she spilled her baby brother's liquid vitamins all over her dress, just minutes after I had finished dressing her for an outing. I had just given the baby, my son Randy, his vitamins and was busily dressing him, when Gina picked up the bottle and pulled off the still-loose cap. The dark, sticky liquid poured down the front of her yellow dress, dripped down onto her white shoes and splattered in odd patterns across a section of the hardwood floor.

When I saw what she had done, I abandoned the half-dressed baby, grabbed Gina up and rushed into the bathroom with her to try to get the dress removed and into water before it was stained permanently.

I was irritated that she had spilled the vitamins, spoiled her dress, interrupted my schedule, and slowed our departure. Grumbling quite audibly, I removed the dress, put it in a basin of water to soak, and began briskly washing

Gina down. In my irritation I looked her straight in the face
and said, "Gina, I could spank you good, girl!"

Her eyes brightened and this very big, self-satisfied
smile lit up her face. She looked at me with this delightful
expression and enthusiastically repeated my last two words,
"Good girl!"

Well, as you might imagine, all my irritation melted
away and I found myself laughing and hugging her instead
of being upset.

That event occurred thirty-one years ago and it is
still as fresh in my mind as ever. It taught me a lesson that
I would be nearly twenty years putting into proper
perspective.

Gina had a very good sense of self back then. Nothing
had happened to her to make her question the reality of her
goodness, so the only thing she heard or saw was what
validated her belief about herself. She was a "good girl" in
her own mind, and certainly in mine, so when my
momentary aggravation didn't fit her image of herself as a
good girl, she managed to shut it out. Neither the irritated
tone in my voice, nor the actual words I spoke, altered her
perception of herself.

We love babies and young children and love to be near
them, because they are so genuine, so full of love and life.
They are so accepting of self and others. They haven't yet
donned the mask that will someday obscure their genuinely
wonderful selves, blind them to their goodness and,
possibly, cause them to lose their way.

But sadly, time and too many unkind experiences have
a way of changing the idealistic images we begin our lives
with. Too often we reach adulthood with a very different
view of ourselves, formed from an assembly of put-downs,
failed attempts, teasing, negative messages, and all the other

hurtful things that have happened to us in our tender, formative years.

Once we have adopted this flawed self-image, our focus changes and now, instead of seeing the wonderful being we were born to be, we see flaws and limitations. Then we begin to look for things that will validate the negative image we now hold of ourselves, and to ignore anything that might invalidate it. We begin to spend a lot of time and energy focusing on and strengthening our perceived flaws and weaknesses. Since other people have always been quick to point these out to us, we think this must be who and what we are. We believe that if we pay enough attention to our flaws, we can keep them in check, which we are certain we must do. We tell ourselves that we must keep our guard up or our flaws may grow bigger and meaner and get completely out of control. If that happens, other people will see how we really are and no one will like us.

Not everyone wears the "I'm flawed" mask. There are those who deceive themselves in the other direction, too. They wear a "pretend I'm great" mask and act as if they are grander than they really believe they are. They adopt an air of arrogance or conceit, and instead of putting *themselves* down, they direct their insults outward, toward others.

Most often though, false beliefs center on negative, undesirable attributes which people claim as their own, and believe themselves powerless to change.

Many people long to be in control of their own lives, but don't believe it's possible. Every circumstance in their remembered past has led them to believe they are powerless. Every attempt they have made to bring their "flawed" selves under control has failed. They seem to sabotage their own efforts and keep running in never-ending circles. They can see the problems, but they have no idea how to fix them. Many aren't even sure they're fixable.

They have generally been searching for answers in every place except the right place, just as I once did. Too often our searches are confined to the world outside ourselves or, if they are focused internally, are focused on perceived flaws. Seeing only flaws, or feeling powerless to change the outside world just makes us beat ourselves up for not being "strong enough" to overcome our "problems."

In my self-esteem workshops, I ask students to list three things about themselves that are special or unique. You would be surprised how many of them have to sit and think for a very long time to come up with answers. Some can't think of even one thing!

Then I ask them how hard it would have been to list three weaknesses or flaws, had I asked for those. They always agree that would have been easy. They are sure they have lots of those. And therein lies the problem. Until we begin to look for our positive attributes, we have little hope of ever finding them. We can't find our strengths while focusing on our weaknesses any more than we can watch the sun rise while facing West.

If you are not sure what your strengths are or what you should be focusing on, start by examining your longings. We may think we *ought* to have certain attributes because other people or societal values tell us we should have them, but we don't *long* for them unless somewhere within us, they already exist, just waiting to be discovered or, more appropriately, uncovered.

Examples of true longing would be a strong desire to express yourself through art or music, or a hunger to become a scientist. Examples of possible "ought-tos" would be thinking you should be more outgoing and sociable than you are, or that you should be more independent. These can be longings, too, if they are internal needs, as opposed to thought-induced wishes. But in America such desires are often the result of the societal values placed on extroverted behaviors and independence. These same desires for someone living in Japan could easily be classified as longings, rather than societal expectations, because in Japan reserved behavior and community, rather than gregariousness and independence, are valued.

What do you long for? What tugs at you, begging for attention or release? I'm not talking about fears, those are products of your negative programs ... of the mask you wear. What I'm asking you to look at is *longing* ... that part of you that says "I would give almost anything to be this or do that."

If You Knew You Couldn't Fail ...

Some wise soul once posed a profound question, which I will repeat here for you to answer. If you *knew* you couldn't fail, what might you try? Most people answer, *everything!* But the truth is, we wouldn't really try everything because there are many things that don't interest us. Take the time now to give that question some serious thought. Don't just answer it in passing. Get a notebook and write out exactly what you would do, if you knew you couldn't fail. You don't have to be realistic at this point. All you need to do is be as sure as you can be that you really want to do the things you list.

It will be helpful for you to start a journal as you work your way through this book. Begin it with the list of *all* the things you think you would try, if you knew you couldn't fail.

As you learn more about your true self, it will be fun and interesting to refer back to this original list. You may discover that your true self led you in the right direction while making this list, or it may be that you based much of it on who you thought you were, rather than on who you really are.

You may want to alter this original list later on, but even so, it will be enlightening. Don't eliminate things you have tried before and failed to accomplish. If you still think you would like to achieve those things, add them to your list.

Give Yourself Permission to Succeed

Many of us are very impatient with ourselves. We think that if we have tried something several times and failed, we must be inadequate in that area. We tell ourselves we are not good at that particular task, and we often prematurely abandon things we once thought we might enjoy. Many people don't understand that humans learn complex skills by practicing them, and that part of the learning process is making mistakes ... lots of them. The mistakes we make in life do not define who we are, they only tell us where we are on the path to perfecting that skill. There is a vast difference between failing at a project or goal and *being* a failure. Failure at a particular thing only means we haven't yet mastered that thing. We haven't given it enough time and attention yet. To *be* a failure means you are incapable of doing a particular thing in any way or at any level of competence, now and forever.

We could say that humans *fail* to fly like birds. We don't have the physical ability to jump from a tower and soar through the air rather than fall. Yet, even here human ingenuity has adapted, and the bolder among us might strap on a hang glider and probably survive that leap. The point is, we need to allow for error if we are to move steadily toward our ideal. To become proficient at anything takes time and effort and there will be many slips and trips along the way. We set ourselves up for failure when we expect flawless outcomes and instantaneous results.

It is especially important to allow room for error when developing complex skills, and many of the skills we need to become fully functioning adults are complex: relating well to others consistently; learning to be assertive; being able to identify and properly ask for what we want in life; knowing and understanding ourselves and others, and applying that understanding in a generally beneficial way. The abilities to communicate effectively, to set and reach goals, to move consistently toward successful outcomes, to function effectively in an ever changing and unpredictable world, these are all complex skills.

Because we tend to learn such things slowly over a long period of time, improvement can be almost imperceptible at times. But improvement does occur, and the average person will eventually achieve a level of true excellence if they are patient enough to persist. Persistence is easier to maintain when we realize that growth is sometimes apparent only when we compare where we are now with where we used to be.

Sometimes we have to look at our own history, the story of our own lives, to learn from our defeats and build on our triumphs. It is especially important that we look at our triumphs and realize that the things we have accomplished and become proficient at over our lifetime did take time and effort.

For instance, none of us was very good at skills like walking and talking in the first year of life. We made lots of mistakes. We kept falling down and we made people laugh with our mispronunciations and incorrect use of words. But because we continued to practice; because we didn't let a few hundred falls or the laughter of others keep us from trying again and again, we got better and better at those skills, and now most of us are really good at them!

Life skills can be compared to skills such as learning to play the piano, learning to speak a foreign language fluently, mastering tennis or golf or dancing. You don't get really good at any of these things in a short period of time. You don't get good at them by reading about them or by observing them in other people. You don't get good at these by simply learning the basic principles involved. You get good by first learning the correct way to apply the skills and then actually practicing them over an extended period of time to perfect them in yourself. Few, if any, skills can be learned by simply observing them, nor can they be mastered without practicing them correctly.

Good practice brings good results, poor practice brings poor results, and no practice brings no results. All the intellectual knowledge in the world won't change the actual results you get, if that knowledge is not put into *continual* practice using the *proper* methods. Mastering life works that way too.

Before we can move in the direction of our ideal, we have to know what the ideal is. Once we know, the passion and dedication needed to persist develops almost automatically. All we have to do then is realize that we will make mistakes along the way, and let that be all right. When we allow ourselves time to practice new skills and develop new ideas, and when we realize that two steps forward and one back is still progress, we can focus on the forward steps and keep moving toward our ideal. The backward steps can help us to discover what we *don't* want and to better define what we *do*. Then, even the backward steps become a form of progress.

Now, let's review the things you'll want to put in your backpack to begin your journey and the things you'll want to leave behind.

Packing for Your Journey

1. Leave behind every false perception you now imagine about yourself, every limitation and every perceived flaw. You can begin by fully examining every major belief you now hold about yourself. Test its validity by asking yourself, "Is it likely I was born with this?" (You were not born with guilt, shame, laziness, lethargy, a poor self-image, most fears, a perception of incompetence, etc.) Then recheck what is left against the facts.

   For example, if you were to check the validity of a fear of people by looking at the facts, you might realize that of the thousands of people you have encountered in your lifetime, most of them were quite pleasant, and very few of them were intentionally mean or vicious. Considering those facts, your fear of people really has little or no validity.

   If you cannot confirm that you were born with your perceived flaws and limitations, if they are of no benefit to you, if you don't like them, or if the actual facts don't completely validate them, leave them behind! You don't need them.

2. Take with you patience, persistence, the willingness to "fail" in order to succeed, an open mind, a willingness to explore, faith that your authentic self is a self you will love and delight in, a certainty that

your ideal path awaits you, and a knowing that once you find your way, your journey will be joyous!

The best way to approach the self-discovery process is as you would a treasure map that you are certain will lead you to a great treasure. Take the time to complete each step along the way before you go on to the next one. Treasure maps have to be followed systematically, you know, or else you might miss an important clue. Know that what lies at the end of this treasure hunt is the self you have been searching for, and the path your authentic self longs to explore.

To add to your store of knowledge in areas where you may want or need more information, I have included at the end of each of the following chapters, where additional information may be required, a recommended reading list. The books listed relate to the subject matter of that particular chapter, enabling you to choose only those titles that are relevant. This allows you to focus your time and attention on areas where additional information may be needed, thereby narrowing your search and speeding your progress.

Before we move on, have you listed all the things you think you would do, if you knew you couldn't fail? If not,... stop and do that now. If you completed that step ... great! Let's move on.

Recommended Reading:

- *I Could Do Anything, If I Knew What It Was,* by Barbara Sher
- *The Seven Habits of Highly Effective People,* by Stephen Covey
- *First Things First,* by Stephen Covey

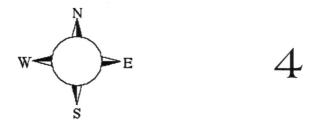

Beginning the Journey

"People are always blaming their circumstances for what they are. I don't believe in circumstances. The people who get on in this world are the people who get up and look for the circumstances they want and, if they can't find them, make them."

George Bernard Shaw

I'll never forget the first time I got up in front of a group of people to present a workshop. I was so frightened that I was literally shaking all over. Fortunately, I had spent the entire night before this presentation either tossing and turning in nervous anticipation, or staring at the ceiling in stark terror, imagining all the things that could go wrong.

Now, normally I wouldn't say that tossing, turning and staring at the ceiling in terror was a fortunate way to spend a night, but I think in this case, it was a good thing, because I was too tired the day of the presentation to shake as hard as my body wanted to.

This was my first self-created workshop. The subject was selling, using a more personal, as opposed to technical, approach. The program was based on the things I had learned the hard way in trying to relate to others well enough to become a good salesperson. This people-based approach had worked well for me. It had taken me from a really awful salesperson (if you could have legitimately called me a salesperson in the beginning) to a very good one.

Although understanding the needs and wants of people and approaching selling from that angle had worked for me, I wasn't sure how useful or necessary this approach would be for other salespeople. And I certainly didn't know how I would handle myself in front of a group. There were eighteen people in that first audience, and I was sure every one of them could see my knees knocking and hear the tremble in my voice. But Gina, my "good girl" who has grown into my dearest friend and business partner, was sitting in the back of the room observing and keeping me on track. To my great relief, she assured me that my fear didn't show. I can only attribute that to the exhaustion from a sleepless night.

I can't say I have never had a case of nervous jitters since then. I've had my share. But today I love teaching and counseling. I enjoy and look forward to doing workshops, and the more people there are, the higher my energy level. I am definitely in my element in front of a group of people. My natural self loves being on stage. But you could never have convinced me of that the first thirty-four years of my life! My mask would have responded ... Who? Me? The shy, passive, insecure, scared-to-death-of-people me ... good on stage? No way!

Sometimes, what seems like the scariest thing in the world can actually be the most beneficial. I can't imagine what my life would be like today if I had never managed to get past all the fears and false self-perceptions that kept me bound to a false image for so long. I would still be trudging my way through sets of numbers as an unhappy accountant, I suppose, instead of delighting in the people I have the privilege to meet through my public speaking, training and consulting.

As it turned out, both my presentation skills and that first program were more than acceptable, but I didn't know that, nor would I ever have known had I not set the fears aside, ignored the perceived obstacles, and continued on anyway.

While we're on the subject of obstacles, I would like to point out one that you may want to get out of your way before continuing on your journey. That obstacle is an incorrect view of failure. Many people allow "failure" to keep them from attempting things they are not sure they can achieve, or to give up on things they don't master quickly or easily. This one obstacle can prevent you from realizing your dreams forever. So, to eliminate the problem, let's look at what failure really is, get it out of the way, and continue on.

Everything we ever succeed at begins with the basics, and involves lots of errors on the way to perfection. In learning to play the piano, for example, we must learn to read music, learn basic fingering techniques, practice the scales repeatedly, etc. We must also be content with one small bit of evidence that we are making progress (scales one day, *Mary Had a Little Lamb* a few weeks later, five or six simple songs in three months, a few "real songs" in six months, etc.). We can't expect to go from the basics to virtuoso in ninety days or even in a year or two. If we do, we set ourselves up for failure.

Actually, there are only two ways to fail. One is to continue on a path that is obviously leading you in the wrong direction. The other is to give up before you reach the goal you want to reach.

An example of the first way to fail is Joe. Joe hated his dead-end job, and dreaded going to work every day. Unhappy and unfulfilled, he lived for the weekend. But Joe hung in there because he was sure that, as long as he played by the union rules, he wasn't likely to get fired or laid off. He was wrong. Seven months before Joe was to retire with full benefits, he got downsized out of a job. He had to accept a seventy-five percent benefits package, which wasn't enough to make ends meet.

Joe spent most of his adult life in a job he hated and then found himself, in his latter years, short of funds. Joe failed because he continued on a course that he knew was wrong for him. His result was not worth the years of misery.

Lana is an example of the second kind of failure. She had been in four serious relationships when she was younger, and in each instance the relationship had failed, leaving her brokenhearted. She decided, after the fourth try, that men were all alike and she was less likely to be hurt if she remained alone. The problem was, she was very lonely and longed to find someone with whom she could form an intimate bond. Lana has not been in an intimate relationship for eighteen years now. She is fifty-two years old and has convinced herself that now it's too late to find love. She continues to avoid situations where she might meet someone.

Lana has failed because she stopped trying to achieve something she really wanted. She will probably die a lonely old woman, because she was afraid to try the fifth, sixth, seventh (or however many) times it might take to find the right life partner.

Do yourself a great favor right now by promising yourself that, if something is important enough to pursue at all, you will pursue it to the end; you will never give up, you will persist and accept as many disappointments and setbacks as necessary to achieve your goal.

The First Step — Developing Self-Reliance

When you step up to the starting line to begin a race, there is no doubt in your mind that you will be the one running it. You have no deluded notion that someone else can run it for you and give you the credit for having won. No one ever questions that succeeding at something as simple as a race requires us to take full responsibility for the outcome, from preparation to crossing the finish line. We are generally aware that "personal improvements," like running a race, begin with self, too, even if we aren't sure what part of self to begin with. But what many people don't realize is that improvements in every area of their lives, including their work, and their relationships must also begin with self.

How well our lives, work and relationships turn out is directly proportional to the level of responsibility we are willing to take for our outcomes. As long as we blame other people and circumstances for the problems we experience in our lives, we will feel victimized by them, and victims feel and act helpless.

For years I blamed my shortcomings on everything and everyone but myself. My over-protective, over-controlling father was the reason I was so fearful and had no people skills. My critical and controlling former husband made me

miserable, kept me from growing up, took what little confidence I may have had from me and made me neurotic. Life
was unfair. It tossed me out into the world without any skills
or money and made me struggle. The world never gave me
a chance. People didn't understand me.

I had an excuse for every shortcoming and each one
seemed legitimate. Nothing I had endured was directly my
fault, in my honest opinion. Wasn't I doing everything I
could to overcome all my disadvantages? Wasn't I reading
and studying diligently in an effort to improve my lot?
Hadn't I stoically held up and kept a stiff upper lip through
all the trials and tribulations that life had visited upon me?
How could any of it have been *my* fault? I was doing my
very best to "overcome" in spite of all the deterrents, was I
not?

In truth, I was not! I certainly *thought* I was, but in no
way was I utilizing the many options I had available to me.
Actually, looking outside myself for the source of my
problems (and thinking I could find them there) kept me
from progressing for many years. As long as I could find a
scapegoat, and as long as I maintained my innocence in the
whole matter, my progress was all but nonexistent.

It's easy to justify any lack of accomplishment when
everything is someone or something else's fault. When we
have deluded ourselves into believing that the blame lies
somewhere, *anywhere* other than right in our own laps, we
can always find a "justifiable" reason as to why things
didn't work out the way we had hoped or planned. And
since the problem is "out there," we seldom bother to look
at ourselves, and we seldom stop to consider what other
options we may have, because if the problem is "out there"
we don't think we really have any options, beyond running
away or fighting back.

We feel stuck, unappreciated, imposed upon, mistreated. We are sure our lives would be absolutely wonderful, except for *them,* those rotten people, those miserable circumstances, all the terrible things that happen to us and that are surely beyond our control.

This belief is the grandfather of all deceptions and self-delusions. As long as we hold onto this belief, we will also manage to hold onto our self-defeating behaviors and, as long as we hold onto self-defeating behaviors, we will meet with defeat! Meeting with defeat, we will feel we are failures and, feeling we are failures, we *are* failures.

I've heard all the arguments over the years, both from myself and from my students. "It really isn't my fault that my parents taught me to be too cautious and fearful. I was just a child. How could I have controlled my parents?" they ask.

It's a legitimate question. We can't change our past, and the fact is, you couldn't have controlled your parents. But as an adult, you are no longer under your parents' rule, and if you continue to cling to old teachings and habits that are no longer serving you well, that *is* your fault. If you have chosen to remain stuck inside those childhood fears, inhibitions, and pain-producing habits into and beyond adulthood, that is *100 percent* your fault.

"But," they argue, "I would love to change those things! I just don't know how! Is that my fault? How can it be my fault that I don't have the skills and knowledge to make the changes I really want to make? I've tried to find the answers. I've tried to develop the skills. What more can I do?"

The answer? I think I'll let you ponder that one. Consider it a "learning self-reliance" exercise. (Hint: Your options grow in direct proportion to your willingness to search the internal depths of your own being.)

"Well, surely it isn't my fault that Jack is so mean and hateful to me," a lost soul persists. "I've tried everything to work things out! He just refuses to cooperate."

No, the way Jack behaves is not your fault. But it is your fault that you continue to deal with Jack in the way you do. It is your fault that you let Jack's behavior upset you. It is your fault that you haven't found another way to deal with Jack's behavior.

"But Jack is family," he complains, "I have to deal with him."

No you don't! You don't have to deal with anyone who is difficult to be around. However, eliminating him from your life should most definitely not be the first choice, if Jack means anything to you.

There are two other options you could try first. The first one is to change your own behavior toward Jack. Quite often when we change the way we relate to another person, the other person will, in time, change the way he/she relates to us. I've seen this happen many times. I have experienced it myself, and have had many people describe such changes.

For example, Allen, a man who attended one of my workshops a few years back, had been fighting and bickering with his wife for more than eight years. They were in the habit of picking at one another, complaining and finding fault. Allen loved his wife, but neither of them made the other happy anymore. I suggested that he purposely and consciously change his approach to her and begin to compliment instead of complain. He didn't see how that would help, but promised to give it a try.

I talked to Allen five months later and this is what he told me: "The first night I decided to try the new approach, Martha had prepared an unusually good dinner and I made a point to compliment her on it But, instead of being pleased, she looked at me suspiciously and asked, 'What's wrong?' I assured her that nothing was 'wrong,' that I just appreciated the good meals she cooked. She still looked suspicious, but said nothing else.

"A few days later, I came home to a freshly cleaned house, which wasn't at all unusual. Martha always keeps the house clean. I had always noticed and always appreciated it, but this time I went into the living room where Martha was and told her how great the house looked, and I bothered to thank her for keeping our home so clean and pleasant. When I told her I appreciated the way she kept the house, Martha got this concerned look on her face. 'What's wrong now?' she asked. Again, I assured her that nothing was 'wrong,' that I just wanted her to know that I appreciated the things she did. This went on for two or three weeks. Every time I noticed something, I made a point of complimenting her and she responded with suspicion. The one-sided compliments must have started Martha thinking, because out of the blue, she began to notice things I did and to compliment me occasionally too. Rather than showing suspicion, I would show genuine appreciation (as you suggested) for her having noticed. Gradually she began to notice and compliment more often and more genuinely and I continued to do the same.

"She eventually stopped reacting with suspicion and soon we were talking about things rather than arguing. We began enjoying our time together like we did early in the marriage. I would never have believed such a positive change was possible. I can't tell you how much it means to me to have our marriage on the right track, and to think it was as simple as taking the time, and making the effort to compliment rather than to complain!"

Relationships are usually good, bad or indifferent as a result of how we act and react toward the other person. If you don't like the relationship you currently have with someone, take it upon yourself to change the interaction by changing your part in it. If the first approach doesn't work, keep trying new and different ones until you get the results you want. If in spite of all your efforts, the other person still maintains his difficult behavior or attitudes, a second option is to determine not to allow that difficult person to affect you. You do that by not placing so much importance on that person's opinions, beliefs and behaviors. When you are fully aware of the fact that someone else's opinions, attitudes or behaviors are of less significance or consequence to you than are your own, then that person can scream, yell and be nasty all he wants and still have little effect on you.

If you can remember a time in your past when someone who meant absolutely nothing to you made some snide or nasty remark, and you either ignored it completely or laughed it off, you know that you can choose not to react when you want to.

The final option is to avoid being around this person as much as possible. This option should be a last resort, but it is an option and you have every right to exercise it, if necessary, to maintain your own peace of mind and happiness.

In fact, when dealing with *any* difficult person, we have only these three options. We can:

1.   Change ourselves, which is the easiest option.
2.   Try to change the other person, which is an impossibility. We can influence change through our own behavior, but we cannot change another person. Each person must ultimately change him or herself (as Martha did) or

3. We can change the environment. That is, get away from the source of the problem.

Obviously the most rewarding option, assuming that the person is worth your time and effort, is to change your part of the interaction by continuing to alter your own responses and reactions until you hit upon the right ones to bring out the best in the other person. Everyone has wants, needs, feelings, and sensitivities that need to be addressed. It may take some time and effort on your part to find them, but if you care about the person and want a good relationship, it's well worth the effort.

Once we start taking responsibility for our problems we discover the options are almost endless. When I began to look to myself, I saw hundreds of options I previously had missed altogether. For example: As a child, I could have chosen to make friends secretly, simply telling my friends about my father's beliefs, so they would know not to call or visit me at home.

I could have chosen to try to understand my father, who was doing the best he knew how, given his own childhood beliefs and lack of understanding. When I finally did come to understand him, and to appreciate him for what he had attempted to do, I could see that what I had seen as suppression and excessive control, he saw as protecting those he loved. Seeing this changed my whole outlook about him, and I learned to love the father I had previously feared and disliked.

I could have chosen to leave home and get a job rather than to marry, and having married, I could have chosen to stand up to my husband instead of letting him control me. Years later he told me that he controlled me to the extent he did because he thought that's what I wanted! My childhood programs that screamed "insecure" possibly did lead him to that conclusion.

I could have made friends during my marriage. We lived in a lovely neighborhood filled with lots of young couples. My former husband was seldom at home. He was often gone for days and weeks at a time. I certainly could have created the opportunity to meet other women with children. Then my three children and I might have all benefited from having new friends. Perhaps the friendships of other women would have sustained me in those "growing up" years and helped me to know myself better. Perhaps, with their support, I wouldn't have felt the need to end the marriage to grow up.

I could have changed my actions and interactions toward my husband and perhaps effected a change in him that would have improved the marital circumstances. Years after we were divorced, I began to relate to him as one adult to another, rather than as child to adult, and from that perspective he can be a pretty decent guy. When viewed from other perspectives, the options were limitless. Yet, for years I lived in pure misery because I believed I had none.

Albert Einstein once observed, "The significant problems we face cannot be solved at the same level of thinking we were at when we created them."

Many of the problems we face as adults are a result of erroneous programs and belief systems we adopted as children. We cannot solve adult problems with the automatic thinking and behaviors of a child. In order to solve adult problems, we must think and behave like mentally and emotionally mature adults. The degree to which you are willing to be responsible for your own life and outcomes is the truest indicator of your level of maturity.

If you read the biographies of great people like Thomas Edison, Benjamin Franklin, Thomas Jefferson,

Albert Einstein, Andrew Carnegie, Margaret Thatcher or Mahatma Ghandi you will discover that they all had two attributes in common: self-direction and a willingness to take full responsibility for their results.

I've heard people say, "Yes, but they lived in easier times," or "Yes, but their lives weren't as difficult as mine," or "They were just lucky." It's easy to find reasons why others have achieved their goals and excuses for why we have not. But excuses never solve problems.

Do you think your life is tough? Do you think you never got any breaks? Do you think you have too many obstacles in your way to be self-directed? Then try reading the biography of Helen Keller, who was deaf, dumb and blind from the age of nineteen months. She lived in total darkness and silence almost her entire life. She never gazed upon a colorful sunset or listened to the fine sounds of a beautiful symphony. Because she could not hear, she never learned to speak clearly, yet she lectured all over the world. She graduated from college with honors and wrote many books. She spent her entire life helping others and was revered the world over. Think of the many obstacles she had to overcome to accomplish those amazing feats. There are many examples of people like Helen Keller who have overcome seemingly insurmountable odds and gone on to excel.

The French journalist, Jean-Dominique Bauby, was left totally paralyzed by a stroke. He was unable to speak or to move, except for blinking one eye. Through that single function, blinking his eye, he and his nurses devised an alphabetical system and he wrote a book which has been hailed by critics as a masterpiece. The book is titled *Le Scaphandre et le Papillion (The Bubble and the Butterfly)*. It is a celebration of life written by a man at a time in his life when he was incapable of speech or movement, and many would say, certainly had nothing to celebrate. He existed, by his own description "like a mind in a jar." Yet, even in that state, he chose to do something important; to make a difference. He struggled long and hard to accomplish a goal intended to benefit his family and humankind in general. He died seventy-two hours after his book had been reviewed and given the great honors it deserved.

What are your limitations? Can you see or talk or hear? Can you move? Do you have a face, hands, feet, legs? There are those who have excelled far beyond the normal, missing one or more of their senses and/or body parts. If they can overcome such odds, what might you be capable of? You will never know until you decide you can and will achieve excellence, and then begin moving consciously and consistently in the direction of your dreams.

The very first step on that proverbial journey of a thousand miles and certainly toward claiming your own greatest treasure, is the step toward self-direction and responsibility. The step that requires you to look directly at yourself and say, "I have been the problem and I will be the solution."

I had a student in one of my workshops who told me that any time she finds herself blaming others for her anger, problems, irritations, or unhappiness, she writes a message to herself and sticks it, via Post-it Notes, on every mirror in her house. Every time she catches her image in a mirror, she sees the message: "You're looking at the problem!" And the sticky-notes stay there until she adjusts her attitude.

It's a great exercise! If you have any difficulty taking complete responsibility for all your outcomes, you might try it. In fact, right now is a good time to put this book down, walk over to a mirror, look yourself straight in the eye and say, "You're looking at the problem!" Take a long, careful look. Then add, "You're also looking at the solution" ... and mean it!

If you did that little exercise, or even imagined yourself doing it, you probably had a small revelation. Understanding that you are the problem and the solution will open more doors for you than you might now imagine.

Deciding now that you are responsible for your own outcomes will be key to succeeding at the remaining steps you will take. Without a willingness to accept the responsibility, you will find a million excuses for not doing the exercises, and a million reasons not to work on the things you know you must. And all you will end up with are excuses.

I took responsibility for my own thoughts, feelings and actions years before I realized I was also responsible for the outcome of my relationships. Once I assumed that responsibility, my relationships improved considerably. It took several more years for me to realize that I was responsible for all my other outcomes, too.

As you begin developing self-reliance, examine every area of your life to determine what adjustments you may need to make to achieve the desired result. You'll be amazed at what you can do and your confidence level will increase with every accomplishment.

As your confidence grows, you'll feel more in control of your life and you'll give up your need to blame the world when things go wrong. When you cease to blame the world, the world will suddenly become a better place in which to live, and the people you encounter will be far more enjoyable to be around. (They'll find you more enjoyable, too!) You'll wonder how solutions that now seem so simple, could have escaped you for so long.

Action Steps

1. Take the time to inventory your life and determine what problems need to be addressed. You may want to start with three or four which you feel are creating the most difficulty for you.

    Your list might include things like always being late, or procrastination or being too disorganized, or maybe things like losing weight and developing an exercise program that you can live with. If you look at your overall life honestly, it won't be hard to decide what to list or give priority.

    As you find and apply solutions to each challenge and check it off your list, the next one will move to the top, and you can address that one. If you start with the toughest one, each time you find a successful solution, the next one up will be easier to solve and soon, solving your problems will be a snap.

2. List each problem or challenge on a separate page in your notebook. (This notebook will become your workbook, so it may be helpful to use a loose-leaf type notebook that allows you to add and subtract pages easily.)

3. Under each problem or challenge, list as many possible solutions as you can think of, even the ones that seem absurd. Sometimes the absurd ones turn out to be the seeds that grow into real solutions.

    If you listed always being late, for example, you could look in several directions for the answer. This used to be a constant problem for me and, in looking for solutions, I listed setting all my clocks and my watch early. I listed writing down my appointments a little earlier than they really were. I listed punishing myself for being late by withholding a reward I'd like to have, and rewarding myself when I was on time.

Ultimately, none of these worked for me. What *did* work was what at first seemed to be among the absurd options, which was to decide why I always chose to be late and try to find a better choice. When I approached the problem as a choice I had made, rather than as an integral part of my nature or a flaw, I realized I was always late because I hated to wait. I also realized that I was inflicting upon others the very thing I hated by making them wait. Since the problem was hating to wait, I realized I could solve the problem by taking something with me to read or work on, in case the other party was late. That way, I wouldn't be idly waiting. I could be doing something I needed to do. The problem was solved and I am no longer chronically late.

4. After you've listed all the solutions you can think of, list the names of people you can talk to, or places you can go to get additional insights, if you feel you need them.

5. Look over the list and pick the best options from among your choices. If you are unsure as to whether or not any of the options you have listed will work, ask someone whose opinion you value, to review them and make recommendations until you get accustomed to developing options you feel confident using.

Be careful not to become overly reliant on this other person and *never* blame them if things go awry as a result of following their recommendations. Remember it was *your* decision to ask the other person and *your* decision to follow the recommendation, rather than trusting your own options, so you still are responsible.

Make it a point to rely on the recommendations of others only as a last resort. Wherever and whenever possible, use your own options. That's the only way you'll ever learn to trust the solutions you create.

The first steps you take as you move away from your old, familiar path may seem a little uncertain and are always the hardest ones to take, even when the familiar path has not been a good one. But your confidence will increase once you know you're headed in the right direction, and each new choice or action will get easier.

It's kind of like taking a really great vacation: the planning, the packing and all the preparations may be a lot of work, but it's quickly forgotten once you reach your destination and start to relax. That's when the fun begins!

Recommended Reading:

- *Emotional Intelligence*, by Daniel Goleman
- *Pulling Your Own Strings*, by Dr. Wayne Dyer
- *Getting Unstuck*, by Dr. Sidney B. Simon
- *Power With People*, by James K. Van Fleet

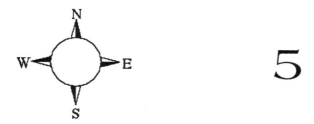

The Search for Self

"I used to think I wanted to be a doctor," Kathy said, "Then I wanted to be a lawyer, but I'm thirty-five years old now. I have a degree in art, which I can do nothing with, and now I'm not at all sure what I should be doing."

When I asked how long she had wanted to be a doctor or a lawyer, Kathy replied that it had been her dream since she was a child.

"Well, why did you get an art degree?" I asked incredulously.

She dropped her head and in a defeated tone she replied, "It was quick and easy, I guess."

There are many people in the world who take the path of least resistance, and at first, this seemed to be what Kathy had done. That turned out not to be the case, however. In truth her nature, her authentic self, had directed her toward something she was not consciously aware she wanted. This is almost as common as taking the path of least resistance. We often take the path of least resistance, simply because we have no idea what we really want. Without knowing, any path will do, so why not take the easiest one?

Sometimes we get lost or confused about where our lives should be headed, because our conscious beliefs about what we should be don't match who we really are. That is exactly what had happened in Kathy's case. She thought she had been lazy or foolish pursuing the art degree. She thought she had been untrue to her desires, and was feeling guilty and useless as a result. She thought she had let her chance for a happy, fulfilled life slip right past her.

But as we worked together to discover her ideal path, an interesting set of facts began to emerge. Kathy's father had convinced her that the only worth people had was in their work, and that only professional people like doctors and lawyers deserved any real respect.

As a child, Kathy had been interested in art, but her father told her that art was a waste of time. No self-respecting person would pursue art, he asserted. Kathy had apparently soaked it all in, and bought every word of it. The only problem was, Kathy loved art! But she also loved her father, and wanted his approval.

When she started college, she chose a school that was about as far from home as she could get, because she "thought she needed to be on her own." It never crossed her mind that she may have needed the distance to pursue her love without her father's interference.

Kathy could have attended almost any university. Her parents were wealthy and willing to pay for her schooling, and in high school Kathy had been an honor student. She was a highly intelligent woman, with an IQ of 158. She could have easily managed to get into a medical or legal program, yet she chose to attend a small university and study art. It didn't take much detective work to figure out why she had taken that route.

Once she could separate her own needs from those of her father, she began building her new life. She had already laid the groundwork, without even being aware she was doing so. All she really needed was an awareness of her authentic self and the realization that she had a right to live her own life and walk her own path. Kathy's path was the path of creativity, because Kathy was, and is, an artist.

Nature and Nurture
The Whole of Who You Are

We can know and understand ourselves more completely by examining the things that have influenced us over the years. These factors all fall into two categories: Nature and Nurture.

Nurture makes up the part of us that we *learned* after we were born and can *re-learn,* if we so choose. Nurture includes everything that influences you in any way, from any place and at any time in your life. Everything about you that was not a natural part of you at birth, everything you believe, and everything you have learned and incorporated into the overall picture of yourself, falls under the category of nurture. Often this is the part of ourselves that we identify with most, especially when early conditioning has hindered the healthy development of our authentic selves.

Nature is the part of us we were born with and will die with. We can function contrary to our nature, but we cannot change it. When we are functioning in harmony with our nature, we are comfortable, happy and content most of the time. When we oppose our nature, in favor of other influences, our feelings can range from mild discontent to downright misery, depending on how far from our natural selves we have strayed.

Determining Your Nature

We will begin our exploration of self with a look at how you perceive yourself. Your perception may or may not match the reality, but either way, it's a great starting point. The basis for the first measuring instrument you will be using has been around for a very long time and has a long history. Early definitions of personality types were presented around 500 B.C. by Hippocrates, the father of medicine.

Hippocrates observed and described four basic behavioral differences in people, which he termed *temperaments.* He suggested these were inborn, genetically determined traits that every person had at birth and which continued to influence him or her throughout life.

He assumed the temperaments had something to do with the *humors,* or bodily fluids, and the names he assigned them were linked to the fluids he believed were dominant in each temperament: Sanguine (for blood), Choleric (for yellow bile), Melancholy (for black bile) and Phlegmatic (for phlegm).

Hippocrates described the Sanguine nature as vibrant, full of life, sociable and friendly. The Choleric nature was described as forceful, confident, bold and decisive. He saw Melancholy as reserved, attentive to detail, withdrawn and moody. Phlegmatic was seen as a slow moving type, who was never in any hurry and seldom ruffled by life's events.

Early psychologists questioned whether "personality" was a product of heredity or environment (Nature or

Nurture), but experts today generally agree that our individual personalities are a combination of both. Most also agree that many of the basic traits described by Hippocrates, are indeed inborn, genetically determined traits that make up a significant part of who we are and greatly influence the directions we take through the nurturing process.

Of course, our bodily fluids are not the determining factors, as Hippocrates believed. Scientists today are exploring the possibility that the variations may have something to do with genetic codes, which are passed onto us much like eye color, and which influence brain chemistry, and there is much evidence in that direction.

Determining Your Nurture

Temperament plays a vitally important role in your general makeup, but it is just one of the many ingredients in your particular personality formula. Most of the other ingredients are products of your environment (Nurture). Those ingredients include your personal preferences, your value system; the "survival" decisions you made while still a very young child; your early programming that came as a result of observing your parents, siblings and other significant people; and the general beliefs and perceptions that you have adopted yourself.

The basis for the instrument you will be using to measure the preferences portion of your personal profile was developed in the early 1900s by Swiss-born psychologist C. G. Jung. In his work he described the various ways different people view the world and process information. Jung identified sixteen possible combinations of preferred behaviors or preferences. Not coincidentally, that number corresponded exactly to the possible combinations described two thousand years earlier by Hippocrates — the four temperaments plus all possible combinations also equal sixteen.

But, where Hippocrates looked at ways of expressing oneself and at reactionary patterns, Jung looked at "functions" and "attitudes." He identified one set of attitudes and two sets of functions. The two attitudes are *introverted* and *extroverted.* The four functions are *thinking, feeling, intuition* and *sensation.*

Jung considered the thinking/feeling functions to be "rational," because they are concerned with comparing and relating things to one another. They are the means by which we make judgments. He termed the intuition/sensation functions "irrational," because they are not directly related to how we make judgments. They are not the awareness itself, but the way in which we process the awareness. The attitudes and functions will be explained more fully in the chapter on preferences.

I began incorporating measuring instruments into my workshops in 1984 using Hippocrates' research on temperaments. Over the years, I realized that though many people fell into the classifications and subclassifications of the basic temperaments, there were many whose personalities did not, on the surface, match the results of their profiles.

Because of my own beginnings, it was apparent to me that something had occurred within their environments to obscure their nature, even from themselves, and to either alter their behavior or their perception of themselves. These people always seemed lost and unhappy, just as I had once been. I wanted a better, more reliable way to help them, so I began to search for other ways to identify and validate natural tendencies.

After years of study and testing various measuring instruments, I began combining the work of Hippocrates and Jung with some of my own. The result is a multi-faceted profile which I call the *C.O.R.E. Multi-Dimensional Awareness Profile* (C.O.R.E. MAP). The C.O.R.E MAP measures both natural and nurtured tendencies, and also defines reactionary patterns, positive to negative functioning ratios, development level of self-recognized traits, and personal effectiveness traits.

We will be examining just two aspects of the C.O.R.E. MAP: temperaments and preferences.

The temperaments profile asks you to look inside yourself and decide what you believe you are (your self-perception).

The preferences section asks you to look outside yourself at the way you see the world, interact with others, and process external information.

These two profiles are then compared to see whether or not your self-perceptions match the way you are functioning. If not, the combined profiles can help you to discover where and why. This is the most valuable tool I have ever seen to help individuals pinpoint areas that need closer examination.

We begin with the temperaments because they represent your core beliefs about yourself. They also point the way to your natural tendencies unless they were altered early in life through negative conditioning.

A good example of how temperaments affect us, especially early in life, can be seen in how a child relates to his or her parents. A child with a temperament that is forceful and self-determined might respond to parental control by fighting back or becoming obstinate, especially in the first four or five years. A child with an easygoing temperament might, in the same situation, go along with being controlled to keep the peace. Another one might actually enjoy the security of being controlled.

Another good way to see the temperaments at work is to watch a young child, one to five years old, in social situations. A naturally gregarious child may be very comfortable and content in the presence of strangers and around a lot of activity, where a more introverted child may cry around strangers and get fussy if there is too much going on. This type of child would be happy playing quietly by himself, whereas the gregarious child would soon be looking for company.

Our preferences, rather than our inborn traits, are what we use to alter or adapt to changing situations. It is our temperament that makes that adaptation easy and pleasant, if it is a complementary adaptation, or difficult and unpleasant, if the adaptation is not complementary. For example, learning to make friends and be sociable is a complementary adaptation for an extrovert and is easy. Being required to be quiet and still in school is not complementary, and so is difficult to learn.

If we are deeply invested in a particular preferential mode, due to its congruence with our natural inclinations, any alteration will be initially uncomfortable and is not likely to occur unless we deem the alteration absolutely necessary to our well being. The longer we function in the opposite preferential mode, the less uncomfortable that mode becomes, but it never feels completely "natural."

To examine that, let's look again at the extroverted child in school. The more talkative, active and unrestrained the child was in the first five years, the more difficult it will be for him to adapt to sitting still and being quiet. It is not uncommon for these children to get lots of reprimands from kindergarten through third or fourth grades. Some even get diagnosed as having an "attention deficit disorder" (A.D.D.). As these extroverted, sociable children are indoctrinated into the school system's structure, however, they learn to conform and sitting quietly becomes less difficult, although it is never as comfortable for this child as it is for the naturally introverted child, for whom sitting quietly is a preference.

We can act contrary to our temperaments, which is exactly what extroverted children are doing when they are sitting quietly, but doing so never becomes a completely comfortable thing to do. We always have to work at being something other than what our natural inclinations dictate.

Preferences can best be demonstrated by looking at hand preference. Almost all people prefer to use one hand over the other. If you are right-handed, for instance, you use your right hand more than your left. You have the ability to use either hand and you often use them both, but you choose or prefer to use the right one where only one hand is required — to eat, write or brush your hair, for example.

If you damaged or lost your right arm and were no longer able to use your right hand, you could use your left hand, but it would feel awkward and your use of that hand would be fairly inadequate at first. Part of the discomfort would be a result of your not being proficient at using that hand, but a greater part of it would be a result of doing something other than what was "natural" for you.

In time however, as you became more proficient at using the other hand, it would begin to feel more natural. You would probably never be quite as proficient with this hand as you had been with the preferred one though. This change of preference would be a *situational* change.

If, however, you purposely chose to use your opposite hand in certain situations, whether or not there was a physical limitation, the change of preference would be *circumstantial.* If you were left-handed, for example, you might choose to learn to eat with your right hand because you attend a lot of banquet-type affairs and don't like bumping elbows with the right-handed people. You may do everything else with your preferred left hand. In this case, the circumstances, rather than your situation, would be what caused you to make a purposeful change, which was not a "natural" one for you, but which served you better.

Usually, when we choose a set of preferences that don't correspond to our natural inclinations, there are either childhood programs that have altered the natural choice, or there are extenuating circumstances in the life of the adult. Understanding the cause enables us to quickly determine what's going on, or to see where some of the contrary childhood programs may reside.

In the years that I have used both the temperaments and the preferences measuring instruments in my workshops, I have discovered that fuzzy or inaccurate results are due to one of three things: (1) The person taking the profiles either does not know him or herself well enough to give accurate answers, (2) they are manipulating the answers in order to appear the way they would like to be, or (3) they are avoiding the correct answers because early childhood programming taught them it was not good to look at oneself in a particular way.

An example of the latter was a young woman I had in a self-discovery workshop. She had an observably bold, extroverted temperament, yet the results of her profile showed her to be timid, introverted, and reserved in manner. Because of the obvious discrepancy, I questioned her results. In so doing, I discovered that her father was a preacher who had taught her all her life that it was "ungodly" for a woman to be bold and outspoken. She had been taught that "good girls" were meek and mild, and it was sinful and improper to be otherwise.

All her life she had been fighting her natural tendencies to be bold, outspoken, driven and confident, because those things were in conflict with her early teaching. As is often the case though, she had not managed to carry the conscious illusion into her unconscious, nonverbal presentation of herself. She was accurately presenting her true nature unconsciously, while very effectively hiding the reality of it from herself at a conscious level. This type of internal conflict will almost always produce ambiguous (and often erroneous) results on the temperaments profile. It also produces confused, unhappy people.

To avoid this type of ambiguity and confusion as you begin to discover your true nature, it is vitally important that you set aside any negative or hurtful beliefs you adopted from your parents and other significant people in your life, and conduct your search based on your own honest needs and feelings.

Setting aside old beliefs is not an easy thing to do. Sometimes it's difficult to determine which beliefs are your own and which ones you borrowed from someone else. Negative conditioning can be so powerful and oppressive as to almost completely obscure an individual's nature. This conditioning creates core beliefs that are almost never questioned, so it can be very difficult for individuals with heavy childhood programming to know what is true about themselves and what is not. People who reach adulthood without really knowing what they want in life or where they should be headed, often fall into this category.

If you were taught never to question people in authority, for example, and to be flexible and easygoing to avoid conflict in your family, you may have grown up thinking and acting like an introvert, even though your nature is extroverted. You may have come to believe that the introverted behavior is genuine, and by adulthood, you just took it for granted, until your extroverted nature began trying to assert itself. When that occurs, you often find you want one thing, but do another, which can become very confusing, causing you to wonder who and what you really are.

If you suspect you fall into the category of being heavily conditioned contrary to your nature, I suggest you answer the questions on the following two profiles as honestly as you can, then answer them again according to your perception of the way you would have to be for you to be totally content. It may help to have others, who know you very well, take the profiles on your behalf as well. Eventually a pattern will begin to emerge.

Which Beliefs are Yours?

The quickest way to determine which beliefs are yours and which ones have been borrowed or bought from someone else is to look at each one that affects your life in any way and ask yourself:

1. Is this belief serving me well in my life?
2. Do I feel good about this belief or does it cause me pain and problems?
3. If this belief isn't serving me well, or if it is causing me pain or problems, why am I holding onto it?
4. How strongly do I really own this belief?"
5. What is the benefit to me of holding onto this belief?

There must be one or you would not be keeping it. For example: Does it keep you from being responsible when things go wrong? Does it keep you "safe" from other people? Does it help you avoid ridicule, rejection, embarrassment?

The beliefs that belong to someone else and which you bought as a child, when you didn't know any better, probably feel uncomfortable. Often they aren't serving you very well as an adult either.

When we buy into a belief as a child, we began to look for ways to validate this "purchase," so we notice things that validate the belief and tend to ignore anything that does not. By the time we are old enough to reason independently, the original belief is so fully validated by selective observation that it isn't even questioned anymore. Superstitions are good examples of this type of selective observation. If black cats equal bad luck, for instance, you will ignore ten great days and focus on the mishap that occurred on the eleventh, because it validates the belief.

The things we buy into as children are generally assigned a place in our unconsciousness quite early, and when these early beliefs surface, they surface as *emotions*. We seldom really examine emotions to see whether or not they are appropriate to our current circumstance or if they are serving us well. What is more important, we usually believe that they are a natural part of us that we can't change even if they aren't serving our current needs.

We seldom examine emotions like frustration or anger, for example. We just tell ourselves we are impatient, or we blame other people for making us mad. If we happen to be shy and afraid of people, we just assume that's how we are. We never stop to question whether the shyness is a learned belief, rather than a natural inclination. We assume the fears, frustrations, and failures are just a part of who we are and must be accepted.

Understand here and now that is not true. You can change *anything* about your psychological makeup that is causing you pain or difficulties. That includes emotions as well as thoughts, beliefs, behavior patterns, habits and values.

Action Steps

1. Examine your basic assumptions and beliefs, recording as many as you become aware of in your journal.
2. Separate a sheet of paper into two sections by drawing a line vertically down the middle of it. Title one side "Keep" and the other side "Toss."
3. On the "Keep" side, list the assumptions and beliefs about yourself, other people, your work, and life in general, that you feel are beneficial to you.
4. On the "Toss" side, list the assumptions and beliefs that create difficulties for you, that you really don't like, or that have no apparent benefit to you.

Note: It's important that you take the time to apply the exercises in each chapter, before you go on to the next chapter. The reason for this is that each exercise is designed to give you a new level of understanding and each level builds upon the other. What you learn in exercise "A" becomes the basis for understanding exercise "B," which becomes the basis for "C" and so on.

By now your journal should have a list of things you think you would like to try, a list of challenges and problems you often encounter, along with possible solutions, and a list of assumptions and beliefs that you may or may not want to keep. If you have all of these, you're doing great! Let's explore further.

Recommended Reading:

- *Change Your Mind, Change Your World,* by Dr. Richard Gillett
- *Reinventing Your Life,* by Jeffrey Young and Janet Klosko, Ph.D.

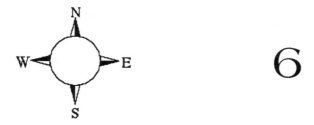

Understanding Your Nature

"If a man does not keep pace with his companions, perhaps it is because he hears a different drummer. Let him step to the music which he hears, however measured and far away."

Henry David Thoreau

What kind of drum beat do you hear? At what pace does it bid you march? Are you the bold, adventurous type who wants to march with quick, steady strides toward the mysteries and challenges of life? Or are you more cautious and conservative? Your beat may be slow and methodical, rather than fast and upbeat, or somewhere in between. Whatever it is, the pace you prefer can provide important clues as to your nature.

Developmental psychologists can identify four basic traits in infants within the first few weeks of life. These four are *bold, timid, optimistic* and *pessimistic.*

The infants identified as "optimistic" are responsive to people in a positive way. They like to be held and cuddled. They smile easily and their natures are light and playful. These babies prefer to be where they can see someone as much as possible. The "bold" optimists grow into gregarious, energetic, playful, talkative little toddlers who never meet a stranger. The "timid" ones grow into shy toddlers who cling to familiar family members, but who are pleasant and easy to care for. Optimistic babies begin responding to human faces quite early.

The infants identified as "pessimistic" tend to be more difficult to care for. They are fussy and demanding, yet they want to be left alone when they are not being fed, changed or cared for in some way. They are not cuddlers, and are less responsive to people than the optimistic babies. Pessimistic babies have a serious demeanor, and seldom smile without some coaxing.

Even the "bold" babies of this more serious nature tend to be less interested in people than the bold, optimistic child. Bold, pessimistic babies grow into toddlers who prefer to take the lead in group activities. If they can't lead the group, they prefer to play alone. They are aggressive toddlers who quickly set personal boundaries. They can be stubborn and difficult when they don't get their way.

The "timid" babies of the pessimistic type are quiet and can seem preoccupied even at a very young age. They grow into toddlers who enjoy solitary play. They can fix their attention on a toy and remain fascinated by it for long periods, examining every detail. They are generally fearful of strangers and prefer to stay home in familiar surroundings.

There is no question that we all have basic temperamental traits that are natural and inborn. But whether your early conditioning or your current adult lifestyle allows your nature to express itself and flourish or not, is another matter.

Those who are expressing true to their nature, are delighted with their lives, their work, their relationships and their "slot" in life.

Some people operate true to their nature in some areas of life, but not in all areas. People often gravitate toward work that more or less suits their basic nature, but may fail to develop relationships and lifestyles that are complementary.

I was so out of touch with myself at the beginning of my search that I malfunctioned in every area. Everything I did, including the work I chose, was a result of adaptation to early conditioning. There would have been no way I could have made any decisions based on my natural inclinations back then. Decisions were fear-based and designed to protect myself from the world and, as you may know, choices based in fear are seldom, if ever, good choices.

No other tool I have found helps people understand themselves and others as effectively as does a working knowledge of the four basic temperaments. They describe distinctly different types of people and these distinctions, once you are aware of them, are readily recognized. Good interpersonal and communications skills may run a close second, but knowledge of the basic temperaments can even help here. I have seen entire families and entire business groups begin to function better and more effectively through understanding and effective application of temperaments. One client applied his new awareness of temperaments to team-building within his organization. He told me that nothing he had tried before had even come close to

giving him the result he was now getting. His new understanding of his people's strengths and weaknesses enabled
him to place employees just where they needed to be to
achieve their highest potential.

It's time now to lay the groundwork for discovering
your highest potential. Begin by taking the temperaments
portion of the C.O.R.E. MAP that begins on the next page.

C.O.R.E. Multi-dimensional Awareness Profile Part 1 — Your Temperament

Instructions

To complete the profile, choose the word that most closely describes you in each of the numbered word sets. In some of the word sets, all of the words may describe you to some extent, and in some none may seem to describe you well. But one of the four will always describe you better or more often than the other three. For example: The words on line one are *resourceful, precise, flexible* and *talkative.* You will choose only *one* of these words. You may feel you are both resourceful and flexible, but you are more (or more often) one than the other. That will be the word you choose. From each line or set, circle the word that best describes you.

In making your choices, think of yourself in an overall context. Try to avoid placing yourself in any particular environment, at work or at home, for instance. Some people are very different at home than at work. So to view either situation exclusively will cause your results to be skewed and will affect the accuracy of your profile.

C.O.R.E. MAP — Part 1 — Temperaments Profile

Circle only *one* word choice from each line — Total the circled words in each column.

	A	B	C	D
1.	Resourceful	Precise	Flexible	Talkative
2.	Adventurous	Thoughtful	Tolerant	Sociable
3.	Persuasive	Persistent	Diplomatic	Fun-loving
4.	Outspoken	Orderly	A Listener	Animated
5.	Decisive	Determined	Friendly	Playful
6.	Confident	Careful	Helpful	Affectionate
7.	Independent	Perfectionistic	Balanced	Optimistic
8.	A Leader	Artistic	Contented	Unpredictable
9.	Bold	Reserved	Patient	Energetic
10.	Daring	Tactful	Obliging	Popular

	A	B	C	D
11.	Competitive	Disciplined	Adaptable	Dramatic
12.	Dominant	Detached	Hesitant	Spontaneous
13.	Tactless	Serious	Indifferent	Forgetful
14.	Intolerant	Rigid	Reluctant	Unorganized
15.	Headstrong	Unforgiving	Doubtful	Inconsistent
16.	Workaholic	Detailed	Undirected	Scattered
17.	Bossy	Nit-picky	Compromising	Restless
18.	Stubborn	Skeptical	Anxious	Changeable
19.	Arrogant	Critical	Timid	Repetitious
20.	Impatient	Resentful	Indecisive	Show-off
	Total ___	Total ___	Total ___	Total ___

After you have totaled each column on the preceding page, place your totals on the appropriate lines below.

Total score for column A _____ Code C
Total score for column B _____ Code O
Total score for column C _____ Code R
Total score for column D _____ Code E

Temperament Type for Column A is Commander (C)
Temperament Type for Column B is Organizer (O)
Temperament Type for Column C is Relater (R)
Temperament Type for Column D is Entertainer (E)

Now, place the code letters (C, O, R and E) on the lines below, with the highest total in the first position, the next highest total in the second position, the third highest in the third position and the lowest total in the last position. If, for example your highest total was in Column D (Code E), you would place an "E" in the first position. If your next highest total was in Column A (Code C), you would place a "C" in the second position, etc.

1 _____   2 _____   3 _____   4_____
  Dominant   Secondary   Backup   Dormant

Combination Types

Most people have clearly defined dominant and secondary types, which make up a combination type. In the case of a combination type, most of your word choices will fall into two of the four categories. Your dominant and secondary temperaments (positions 1 and 2) are generally the ones that you use. Your dominant temperament is the one you use most often, and to which you probably relate most. The secondary temperament modifies the dominant one in the direction of the secondary. The closer in strength the secondary and dominant temperaments are, the stronger the modification.

True Types

A small percentage of people (about six percent) dominate one temperament almost entirely, so that the total of one column is considerably greater than the other three totals combined. These are considered true types. True types behave very true to the description of that one particular type, where combination types display some mix of the dominant and secondary temperaments.

Blended Types

Occasionally, someone will have more than two columns that have fairly close, or even tied, totals. Where three (or all four) columns are close, you are using opposing attributes somewhere, which means that neither of the opposing temperaments is well developed. Someone who has close or equal scores in introverted and extroverted temperaments, for example, hasn't developed either of these traits sufficiently.

This is considered a blended type, and is most often seen in people who don't know themselves well. Generally, as those with blended results learn to know themselves better, they will tend to move toward one or two of the temperaments, becoming a true type or a combination type.

Oppositions

An opposition occurs when two opposing temperaments occupy the dominant and secondary positions. This is
usually a result of the effects of nurturing, rather than a
natural effect. This effect tends to disappear as the individual begins to develop the natural self and move away
from the effects of early influences. The oppositions are
Commander/Relater or Relater/Commander and Organizer/
Entertainer or Entertainer/Organizer.

Are You Self-Aware?

The blended types and the oppositions often indicate
a lack of self-awareness, but this is sometimes true of those
who test as Relaters, as well. Adaptations to early nurturing
that have caused us to suppress our natural inclinations can
push us in the direction of passive, flexible behaviors that
can simulate the Relater style. The way to tell if a Relater
result is a true one is to read the description for Relater and
see if it suits you. If it does suit you and *you are happy and
content with that fact,* it is a true profile. If you aren't partic-
ularly content to be a Relater type, it's probably a nurtured
effect.

There Is No "Best" Type

With the exception of oppositions and blends, which
indicate that you have not yet developed your genuine self,
there is no one temperament type or combination of types
that is any better or worse than any other type or combination of types. They are simply different. Each type and each

combination has its own uniqueness, its own strengths and weaknesses, and each one has something special to contribute to the world. Discovering your particular temperamental type or combination will be one of the most helpful and useful things you will ever do. Knowing your strengths and weaknesses will help you to focus more clearly on the attributes you would like to develop.

Knowing why you pursue certain things and avoid others can lead to greater self-acceptance. For example, maybe you adore parties and social occasions, or maybe you hate them. You may love attending to details, or you may find them difficult and frustrating. You may work hard at building good relationships or you may prefer to build a business instead. When you understand that certain behaviors, certain likes and dislikes are perfectly natural, you don't let them worry you anymore. Plus, if you don't like certain natural tendencies, you can keep them in check better when you are more fully aware of them.

The same holds true in your relationships. Whether you enjoy people or just tolerate them, you will better understand why. You will know why you get along well with certain types of people and not with others, and you will know how to alter your behavior to suit the person you are dealing with if you so choose.

In order to get the most from your profile, it is very important that you answer the questions honestly. If there's any doubt in your mind as to whether or not you answered with total honesty and accuracy, go back and re-take the profile before proceeding any further.

Don't be too concerned initially if, after reading the descriptions of the four temperaments, you are not sure you fit your profile. Most people are immediately aware that, "Yes, that's definitely me!" A few, however, are not sure.

If I had taken this profile twenty years ago, I probably would have tested as a Relater, because my adaptations to early nurturing had caused me to act totally foreign to my nature. This is often true of people who are raised by a domineering, controlling parent.

When both parents are controllers, a fairly high score in Relater is especially likely. That holds true whether the child was controlled openly through aggression and punishment, or covertly through manipulation and guilt tactics.

If you typically act a certain way, (shy and withdrawn, for example) but are uncomfortable with those actions (uncomfortable, not necessarily unhappy) you are probably acting contrary to your nature. Introverted types are sometimes unhappy with the way they are and would like to be more extroverted and outgoing, but they are not uncomfortable being introverted. They would be uncomfortable trying to be extroverted, even though they think they would be happier with themselves if they were more outgoing.

A true extrovert, on the other hand, would actually be uncomfortable maintaining a shy, withdrawn position, and would only assume such a posture consistently as a result of negative influences in their upbringing.

An important part of understanding yourself is in realizing that it's okay to be a certain way (introverted for example). It is also good to know that, if you choose to act differently than what your nature dictates, you can do that, although doing so will require some effort on your part, and may never be completely comfortable. When you understand this up front, you can decide whether you want to follow your natural inclinations and enjoy yourself as you are, or choose the different route. When you are fully aware that the alternate route may mean learning to live with some self-imposed inner-tensions, it's easier to achieve the desired result, because you know what to expect.

Say, for example, that you are naturally introverted but you want to be a public speaker. If you understand up front that public speaking, or anything else that requires you to interact in an extroverted way, will require extra work on your part and will always feel slightly uncomfortable, then you will be prepared for that result. Being prepared, you will have a far greater chance of approaching the task realistically and succeeding at it.

If, on the other hand, you are an extrovert by nature, but you want to carry on your father's accounting business, you will be far more likely to succeed if you realize that accounting will require extra amounts of discipline on your part. Again, knowing up front will help you to prepare yourself for the extra measure of discipline required. Or you may realize that you can best run the accounting business by hiring more introverted, detail-oriented people to do the actual accounting, while you go out and sell new accounts or improve customer relations.

Natural inclinations and limitations don't prevent us from doing things that are not "natural" for us, but we do have to work harder to excel in "unnatural" areas. If it's important to you to do something different than what is natural for you, however, go for it! Just be prepared to work a little harder than those whose natures incline them to such things.

To understand how being one type and acting like another can cause discomfort, look again at the career choices I made initially. Remember the waitress job I hated so much, and my decision to go into accounting? Because I was operating out of fear and negative conditioning rather than self-understanding, I thought accounting would be a perfect career for me. In truth, I found the detail, the repetition, the predictability and all the other elements common to accounting, terribly boring. I hated the monotony, and I had a terrible time justifying spending two hours looking for a nickel so the books would balance. Every year, I became more and more dissatisfied until, finally, I found the work so unpleasant that I had to look for alternatives.

If I had to choose between being an accountant or a waitress today, income potential being equal, I would choose to be a waitress without hesitation. Why? Because today I understand myself and I know that waitressing comes closer to fulfilling those needs than does accounting.

My Commander/Entertainer nature gives me a primary drive (or need) to be in command of things — to call my own shots, to seek challenges, to be innovative and active. My secondary need is to interact in a social way with people. This combination doesn't like details at all. While being a waitress requires some attention to detail, it sure doesn't require as much as accounting. Accounting doesn't allow for much interaction with people either, where waitressing is filled with it.

Based on my natural inclinations, accounting was about as poor a choice as I could have made. I would never have chosen that profession had I been in touch with my nature. That I soon grew to dislike it is a very predictable outcome for this temperament combination.

If you dislike your work, or any other aspect of your life, it's quite probable that the area you are unhappy with requires you to act contrary to your nature.

Read the following descriptions of the four basic temperaments and see if you recognize yourself. Chances are that your results will be amazingly accurate, but if they aren't, there are other areas of your life you will want to explore before you retake the temperaments profile.

There are positive and negative types described in each temperament overview. If you tend toward the positive, you probably won't recognize yourself in the negative. You aren't supposed to. Negative types are quite different from the positive ones. Positive people of any type are valuable assets to family, friends and societies. Negative ones of any type usually mean trouble.

Discover Yourself First

Each temperament is presented in its own chapter to enable you to go directly to the ones that match your dominant and secondary temperaments. You may want to read and familiarize yourself with all of them eventually, to better understand and relate to other people; but for now, focus on the chapters that will help you to understand yourself better.

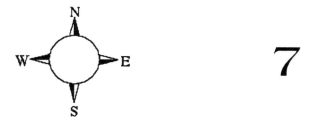

7

The Commander
(originally Choleric)

Who's the boss? The Commander, of course. At least that's what he thinks and how he acts. Even children of this nature try to run the show.

My first grandson, Bryan, has a Commander nature and he was running the show before he was a year old. If he wanted to talk to you, he insisted you get down on the floor so you would be on his level. You don't talk down to Commanders. When Bryan set his mind in a certain direction, his parents had to go along with it, reason him out of it, or prepare themselves for a real battle. True to his nature, Bryan did not like taking "no" for an answer, though he was quick to say no.

Bryan is nine years old now and he still knows exactly what he wants. He is decisive and loves the idea of working. He has always been the most cooperative and contented when working side-by-side with a family member. His secondary temperament is Entertainer, so he enjoys people too.

At the age of six, Bryan was selling lemonade at his own lemonade stand. Gina, his mother, made a little sign that said "lemonade, ten cents" and taped it to the front of the stand. No matter ... Bryan managed to talk about half of the customers into giving him more than ten cents. Sometimes he got as much as fifty cents. What a salesman!

By eight, Bryan thought he needed a job. His "official" title at our company is "Executive Assistant." He makes a whopping two dollars an hour when he helps out. But, for Bryan, the money isn't what's important. I think he's grooming himself to take over the business!

General Commander Traits

Commanders are natural extroverts; bold leaders who prefer to run the show, lead, be at the helm. They seek success, but what constitutes success may vary from one Commander to the next. No matter how they define it though, Commanders move toward success with unrelenting determination. Once they set themselves in a direction, it is almost impossible to dissuade them or to alter their course. They will achieve their goal or die trying. Commanders are highly motivated and can persevere long after others would have given up. Of the four temperaments, none are as driven or self-directed as the Commander. They are the players in life. They would much rather be doing than watching. "Lead, follow or get out of the way" is the Commander's general approach to life.

Commanders are decisive, self-motivated and determined. They can see the big picture and are prone to dream big dreams. They are *action* people who like to get things done. They have a strong need to be in control and they chafe at the idea of having to subordinate themselves to anyone. If it is at all possible, Commanders will find some way to gain control of at least some area of their lives. Commanders who are stifled and controlled at work, for instance, can be real control freaks at home.

All Commanders have a strong desire to gain and/or keep a considerable degree of control over their own lives, but negative Commanders aren't content to just control their own lives. They also want total control over the lives of everyone around them, of circumstances, even of the whole world, if that were possible. Positively inclined Commanders just want to be sure they have control of themselves.

Unlike Entertainers (the other natural extroverts) who can talk your leg off, Commanders don't care for trivia or small talk. Whereas Entertainers can expand a story to eight times its original size by adding color and elaborating endlessly, Commanders want to get through it as quickly as possible. To do anything less is a terrible waste of time and energy, as far as they are concerned. "Get to the bottom line," is one of their favorite statements.

Because Commanders are natural leaders, no one has to push them to get them moving, unless negative nurturing has altered their natural inclinations. Pushing a Commander is about the worst way in the world to get them to comply. They become instantly obstinate when pushed. The best way to get something done by a Commander is to challenge him or her. Commanders love a challenge!

The way to get Bryan directed and motivated, for example, is to set him a task and tell him how hard it is for most children his age to accomplish such a task. He will work like crazy to achieve the goal. He usually does it, too, and then he almost visibly swells with pride.

Commanders are good at delegating tasks to others, provided they are not the over-controlling types. Negative (over-controlling) Commanders want to have a hand in everything and seem to believe that there isn't another competent soul on earth beyond themselves, so they must either oversee everything or do it themselves. They can waste a lot of time and energy that way.

Positive Commanders are quite happy to delegate, and they are good at it too. They realize that by delegating they can use their energies to keep the enthusiasm of everyone on the project high enough to accomplish even the toughest of jobs. They are great motivators who lead fearlessly. They back down from next to nothing. Difficult and dangerous situations that would send others scurrying in horror or cringing in fear seem to activate the Commander. They just jump in and handle it ... no big deal ... piece of cake!

Commanders are confident, outgoing and enthusiastic. Whereas Entertainers concentrate their energies on social pursuits, Commanders concentrate theirs on succeeding. Entertainers adore entertaining people just because it's fun; Commanders tolerate social situations only if they can see some value (success-wise) to the association. What Commanders generally call "friends," other people would call "business associates."

Commanders are the adventurers, the daredevils, the forceful powerhouses of the world. Theirs is the image that is held up to Americans as the ideal for the business world.

Interestingly, both the social ideal (Entertainer) and the business ideal (Commander) are reported to be minorities among the temperaments. According to research done on just one aspect of profiling, true Entertainers make up only fifteen percent of the population and true Commanders only twelve percent. I suspect a large number of those who test as introverts have been conditioned in that direction, but even so, you can imagine why so many people (seventy-three percent to be exact, for you Organizers) are struggling to live up to American ideals.

The Commander's focus on action and success can make them seem uncaring or disinterested in people. They aren't, really. They just get caught up in achieving their goals and forget to do the little things that let others know they care. Commanders are thinking, as opposed to feeling, types and their idea of showing affection often falls into the category of logic. Their logic goes something like this: "If I care enough about you to spend precious time with you, if I am willing to work hard for you, if I allow you to share some portion of my life, how can you possibly think I don't care about you?" That may not be very romantic or reassuring, but it is often the best you will get once the honeymoon is over and the Commander gets back down to business.

Commanders seek power, expediency, victory, success and control. Lack of these things can lead to stress, and since the world doesn't always step aside and let them through, Commanders are prone to the tensions that are a result of not always being able to charge ahead at the rate they would like to.

Once they learn to roll with the punches though, positive Commanders get a lot done. They are dynamic, directed, helpful, decisive and amazingly effective. People are energized and directed by positive Commanders, who are real motivators and outstanding leaders.

Some Negative Traits to Watch For

If you are a Commander, you will benefit greatly by looking at yourself closely. Commanders are the least likely of the temperaments to admit to any shortcomings, but are the quickest to correct them once they are acknowledged.

Among your possible shortcomings are the tendencies to be too controlling at times, too bossy, and too blunt and to-the-point. Commanders often expect too much from non-Commander types. You may have head-on clashes with other Commander types because both of you want to be captain of the ship. Commanders sometimes dream big dreams to the point of going overboard and forgetting to be cautious. They prefer to look at the big picture and ignore the details, which could prove to be quite problematic at times. Commanders can become so preoccupied with becoming successful that they forget to find pleasure in the present moment!

Really negative Commanders can be downright scary. In fact, of all the temperaments, none is as extremely different at the positive and negative ends of their natures as are Commanders.

Negative Commanders are bullies. They order or push people around, try to control everything and everybody, and have no problem doing whatever it takes to get what they want, including arguing, intimidation, sabotage, fighting, punishment or purposely inflicting emotional or physical pain. They are bulldozers who will doze over anyone or anything they think stands in the way of their getting what they want, and no one is immune. They can bully, intimidate and abuse spouses, children, co-workers, acquaintances, strangers and even friends, if they have any.

Negative Commanders don't usually have friends, though. They are feared and disliked by almost everyone.

To Be an Effective Commander

1. If you are a Commander, you probably need to lighten up! Allow others to move at their own paces. Don't expect others to be as driven as you are. No other temperament is.

2. Trust other people to handle things for you sometimes. There really are other people in the world as capable as you. Relinquishing control occasionally will not only make the people around you happier, it will make your life happier and more effective too. After all, what you really want is good outcomes and achieved goals. Other people can help you accomplish these much faster, if you let them.

3. Understand that you were born to be a leader, so lead, don't push!

4. Stop driving yourself so relentlessly. Learn to enjoy the process. Getting there is really ninety-eight percent of the fun. Besides, once you actually arrived, what would you do? You'd be bored to tears doing nothing. Leisure really isn't your bag, no matter how much you try to convince yourself it is! You would last about a month (if that long) lazing around, then you would simply have to do something. You would have to go out and find a new challenge. Challenge is what makes your life exciting. So, enjoy the journey. It's what you're all about.

5. Practice showing other people that you care about them as people. You can get so caught up in your

successes or efforts to achieve, that you forget to show other people how important they are to you. People cannot read minds. They need to be told that they are loved and appreciated. This may not feel natural for you at first, but once you start doing it, it will get easier and you will love the results.

Some Good Career Choices for Commanders

Commanders are good at many things, but they really shine in places where they have a lot of latitude and can usually call their own shots.

Some good choices are:
- Chief Executive Officer
- Upper-Management Positions
- Entrepreneur
- Business Owner
- Sales
- Marketing
- Medical Doctor
- Dentist
- Trial Lawyer
- Legal Advisor
- Investment or Mortgage Broker
- Stockbroker
- Business Consultant
- Coach
- Office Manager

Commander Overview

Tendencies
- Bold
- Direct and Decisive
- Innovative
- Risk Takers
- Goal Oriented
- Acts with Authority
- Accepts Challenges
- Good Problem Solvers
- Status Conscious
- Appears Powerful or in Control
- Takes the Lead

Needs
- Action
- Results
- Accomplishment
- Sense of Control
- Efficiency

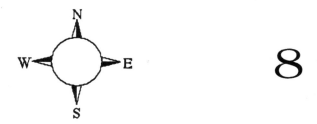

8

The Organizer
(originally Melancholy)

- -

There are two types of Organizers: the sensitive, compassionate, artistic type; and the numbers, charts, attend-to-details type.

Almost all of our great artists, composers, poets and musicians have either been true Organizers of the first type or have had Organizer as a large part of their combination type. This type of Organizer is still precise, meticulous and perfectionistic like the numbers type Organizer. They still want order and predictability, and they are willing to attend to details (to some extent), but they don't necessarily like dealing with numbers and statistics the way the other type does.

My oldest son, Randy, is an Organizer of the first type. He is currently working on his Ph.D. in biology. His professional choice should have been a surprise to no one, because from the time he could walk, he was gathering up injured birds and animals and bringing them home to heal. When Randy wasn't rescuing wildlife, he was drawing it and he became an outstanding artist and sculptor. His exceptional talents had everyone expecting art to become his life passion. But, no ... the animals kept calling to him, and his great compassion for the perceived plight of the animal kingdom won out over his natural and considerable art talents.

Tom, my accountant, is an Organizer, too. He isn't especially worried about the animals of the world. His interests lie in keeping people organized at the accounting level. Where Randy is intense and dramatic, Tom is very reserved and subtle. Everything in his office is perfectly ordered. Even his desk is perfect, which I find hard to understand. How do you get paperwork done with a perfectly clean desk?

Tom is methodical and thorough and, of course, so is Randy; as a scientist he has to be. But Tom approaches things from a different angle. He loves making numbers work for him and his clients. Randy has little interest in numbers beyond how statistics affect his work. To Tom, numbers are everything; they *are* his work. He loves to attend to small details. This intense love of detail is almost exclusive to the Organizer. It cannot be seen to any extent in any other temperament. The second type of Organizer loves charts, graphs, statistics, exact percentages, and lots of detail.

You don't dare ask an Organizer of either kind a question when you're in a hurry. They really don't like giving short, brief answers. "What time is it?" brings you a history lesson on how time came to be measured. The answer to "What are you doing?" could take up an entire afternoon! Even when they keep their answers brief, they have to be more specific than most of us require.

Ask an Entertainer or a Commander how much something costs and they will answer, "Oh, about fifteen dollars." Ask an Organizer and you'll get, "Fourteen dollars and thirty-nine cents, plus tax; which would be a dollar, fifteen; that would make it fifteen dollars and fifty-four cents." See what I mean about having a problem getting short answers?

General Organizer Traits

Organizers are precise, proper, meticulous, and very orderly. I have had a number of Organizers in workshops who were very proud to relate to the class how they keep all their socks, shoes, shirts, underwear, etc., folded neatly in drawers or hung precisely in closets and arranged according to clothing type, color, fabric, etc. That level of order would drive most of us absolutely crazy. True Organizers thrive on it.

The numbers and statistics type of Organizer can get absolutely giddy over such things as algebra, trigonometry and calculus. Getting a complicated set of books to balance to the penny is as exhilarating to this type of Organizer as a trip to Disneyland would be to the average child.

Even though the artistic type of Organizer isn't quite so enchanted with numbers and statistics, they can do some real exciting and artistic things using charts and graphs! Actually though, they would rather be writing great poetry, taking breathtaking photographs, painting beautifully detailed pictures, creating intricately detailed sculptures, writing hauntingly beautiful musical scores or creating marvelous, perfectly arranged homes and gardens. Even their garages are clean, orderly and artistically arranged, as a rule!

Both types of Organizers are cautious. They look very carefully at all the angles before they will make a decision and, if everything isn't in precise order (in their opinion) they will refuse to commit. They use this same cautious approach when making friends, choosing a job or profession, and in anything else they consider of long term importance or consequence, which is just about everything! This level of caution can be very useful when it's applied in a positive manner. Many a Commander has been saved from one or more headlong plunges into disaster (which Commanders have a knack for diving into) by a cautious Organizer who anticipated trouble in time to divert or avoid it.

Some Negative Traits to Watch For

On the negative side, Organizers can move toward too much caution, which can keep them stuck in one place, unwilling to make a move of any kind for fear of falling short of perfection. Perfection is, of course, nothing more than a perception and can never really be achieved. What is perfection to one person may not be to another. To constantly pursue perfection has a way of making life more difficult rather than more pleasant, but you can't tell that to an Organizer bent on perfection.

Negative Organizers can spend so much time checking and re-checking every detail that they become ineffective. They can bore and irritate others with their insistence on explaining everything in great detail, even when others are begging them to get to the point.

Negative Organizers can be very critical and intolerant of others as a result of their overly high expectations. They often seem distant and aloof. They have a difficult time expressing their feelings or complimenting others, so those around them generally hear only complaints and criticisms. Negative Organizers are often described as Snipers:

those passive/aggressive types who love taking potshots at people, and putting them in difficult or embarrassing positions to watch them squirm. They can also be excessively critical and caustic.

To Be an Effective Organizer

1. Stop chasing perfection and learn to pursue *excellence* instead. Excellence can be achieved, measured and evaluated properly by others, as well as by oneself. It's a much healthier and more readily attainable goal. The problem with perfection is that even if you think you have achieved it, the longer you look at it, the less perfect it appears. And you are forced to continue *ad infinitum* striving to achieve it.

    The quest for perfection and the refusal to settle for anything less, has caused many an Organizer to sit immobilized, accomplishing nothing, because rather than do something less than perfectly they would rather do nothing at all. This is a sure formula for failure, so lighten up! Realize that before you can get to "perfection," whatever you think that is, you have to work your way past all the imperfections. Allow yourself the luxury of making mistakes, of being less than perfect, in order to reach your ultimate goal of excellence.

    Organizers have the capacity to do some outstanding things if they can learn to be more accepting of the less-than-perfect results that are a necessary part of the learning process and to let go of the frustrations that cause them such grief when things are less than perfect.

2. Organizers tend to expect a lot from themselves and from others. These expectations can appear to others as criticism. Learn to accept others as they are and stop trying to change them to suit your image. The world is not all black or white. Learn to look at, and allow for, other options. You will be a lot happier if you are not so hard on yourself and on others.

3. Realize that most other people are not as detailed and meticulous as you are, and that's good! If they were, they wouldn't need you so much. Learn to fill in the gaps for others and attend to the details you love without expecting others to do the same for you. If you can put aside the tendency to be critical, you can be a real asset to the rest of us and we'll love you for it. My husband and all three of my children have Organizer traits and I don't know what I'd do without them helping me to keep my life orderly and on track.

4. When you care about someone, learn to tell them so. Organizers can be hard to read, and they tend to think those they care about should know how they feel, without being told. Seldom is this true. So, rather than take any chances, express how you feel. This may seem a little unnatural for you at first, but if you keep it up, you'll love the results.

Some Good Career Choices
for Organizers

Organizers excel in areas where attention to detail and meticulousness is important. They like structured environments and don't mind working within a hierarchical system.

They tend to dislike work and environments that lack order, precision and predictability.

Some good choices are:
- Accountant
- Bookkeeper
- Office Manager
- Administrator
- Computer Analyst
- Programmer
- Data Entry
- Word Processing
- Efficiency Analyst
- Estate Planner
- Credit Analyst
- Scientist
- Insurance Underwriter
- Bank Examiner
- Securities Officer
- Law Researcher
- Legal Secretary
- Pharmacist
- Administrator
- Lab Technologist
- General Surgeon
- Veterinarian
- Engineer
- Mechanic
- Technical Writer
- Teacher (Math, Science)

Organizer Overview

Tendencies
- Detailed
- Precise
- Analytical
- Perfectionistic
- Controlled
- Cautious
- Systematic
- Orderly
- High Expectations of Self and Others
- Wants Lots of Facts
- Appears Reserved and Serious

Needs
- Stability
- Order and Logic
- Certainty
- Details and Facts

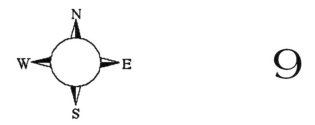

9

The Relater
(originally Phlegmatic)

Linda's family is her life. She spends nearly every waking minute chauffeuring her children around, making sure the house is clean, everyone's clothes are clean and pressed, and nutritious meals are on the table. This is not an uncommon practice for stay-at-home mothers, but Linda loves it. She is also active in her church, where everyone thinks she is a real saint ... and she almost is.

Linda is my sister. The entire family adores her. She is the quintessential hostess, no matter how often you visit her. Even when the entire family converges upon her for a family reunion, she is calm and congenial. Most people would fuss and worry over a house full of family members, with all their children running everywhere, but not Linda. She stays cool, calm and collected. Everyone feels right at home and very welcome in Linda's presence.

About the only time her feathers get ruffled is when someone tries to hurt or take advantage of someone she loves. Someone can pick on Linda all day and pretty much get by with it, but let them try to hurt one of her loved ones and she can come out fighting like a gamecock. But, true to the Relater type, fighting is most definitely not Linda's way. She will do almost anything to keep the peace and to build bridges in relationships. Linda is a positive Relater.

General Relater Traits

On the positive side, Relaters are seen as true saints. They are so easygoing and relaxed about life, so forgiving of the shortcomings of others, so easy to talk to. They exude genuine compassion and concern for others. People flock to them because they are so caring and understanding. They are great listeners, who will sit for hours and let you cry on their shoulder. They will offer solace and helpful suggestions. They will even do for you what needs to be done to make you happy, sublimating their own wants and needs to satisfy yours.

Relaters are kind, gentle, generous, caring, concerned, flexible — in short: saintly people, on the positive side. Relaters do have a negative side as well and their negatives can be just as frustrating to other types, and even to their own types, as their positive traits can be delightful.

To Relaters, relationships are the most important things in the world. They will do anything to avoid problems with other people. This fact makes them quite lovable and helpful most of the time, but it can also make them quite difficult to deal with at times. That's because they would rather not make any decisions that might offend anyone, which can make them very indecisive. The indecisiveness doesn't always present a problem. In fact, initially it can seem a quite pleasant trait, because the other person always gets his or her way. Eventually, however, always having to make all the decisions and then watching the Relater sulk silently, when what you decided isn't what he or she had really hoped you would decide, can get to be a problem. At that point, the more decisive types (especially the Commander) begin to insist that the Relater make some of the decisions, and when they decline to do so, trouble begins to brew. Of course, this only makes the Relater work harder to keep the peace and, in the process, they build up a lot of personal tension.

Relaters handle tension by withdrawing, which causes those who are accustomed to the Relater's warmth to begin to worry. This cycle can continue to feed upon itself until someone, usually the other person, breaks it. It's usually the other person, because the Relater can't decide what to do.

Non-Relaters can quickly identify a Relater by asking them almost any question that requires a decision. Something as simple as, "Where would you like to go eat?" can tie up an entire afternoon if you wait for the Relater to decide. The indecisiveness can drive the average person wild, but the Relater actually thinks they are being agreeable rather than difficult. And the fact of the matter is, for the most part, they really don't care what they do or where they go as much as they care about pleasing others and avoiding any unpleasantness. The problem is that, on the occasions when they do care, they don't say so and then get upset because we fail to guess right.

Another problem is that, although Relaters may feel unsure of themselves, they often appear to be strong, capable and all-together. They never ask for help, even when they desperately want it, because they don't want to put anybody out. Because they appear strong and together and because they never ask for help, we assume they never need anything, so we don't offer help. When that all together look is a facade to hide the pain and insecurities which often plague Relaters, and we fail to recognize that, Relaters get their feelings hurt and get obstinate. Then they withdraw and the rest of us don't have a clue as to why.

If you are a Relater and find yourself going through life with your wants and needs unmet by others, realize that you are creating that problem by looking so capable and unflappable on the surface and by never letting anyone know you have wants and needs, too. Learn to ask for assistance, and to receive as well as you give. It's an art and a real challenge for you, but work on it.

One of Relaters' strengths is that they are flexible enough to be able to move into any of the other roles for a short period of time, if necessary. Granted, the role of Commander is an uncomfortable one for Relaters and they would prefer to avoid that one, but more than all the other temperaments, Relaters have the flexibility to move from one attitude to another long enough to achieve a desired result. No other temperament is laid-back and easygoing enough to deal with the tensions of moving back and forth. Their flexibility and easygoing way can be a real asset if applied wisely.

Like the Organizer, the Relater is an introvert and would prefer to stay in the background. Like the Entertainer, the Relater loves people, but rather than wanting to be the center of attention, the Relater would prefer to sit back and just watch. In fact, Relaters would really prefer just to watch in just about every area of life. They tend to be spectators more often than participators in life, except in the area of helping others. When it comes to building relationships, no one outdoes the Relater.

Some Negative Traits to Watch For

Negative Relaters are extremely indecisive. So much so that not only do they drive the more decisive types up a wall, they are also a real problem to themselves. They simply cannot make a decision, and they aren't very happy about the decisions others are forced to make for them either.

In the assertiveness classes I teach, the most passive types are almost always in the Relater group. Their passivity causes them a great deal of inner conflict and pain. They keep trying to please others and others keep running roughshod all over them. The harder others push, the more the Relater withdraws, and soon they are backed into a corner and don't know how to get out. The result is tension, emotional pain and fear. They hold the tension in until it builds too high to contain any longer and, when they finally release it, they explode in a rage. The angry outburst usually embarrasses and worries them. They can't imagine what came over them. They usually take the blame for the outburst upon themselves and feel bad about it. Then they quickly regain their composure and go back to their normal, gentle selves until someone pushes them too far again. They usually respond to this type of passive, then explosive, behavior with guilt, shame and self-castigation.

Their tensions probably wouldn't run so high as to lead to even occasional explosions, if Relaters didn't spend so much more time giving than receiving. They can't understand why they can see and anticipate the needs of others so easily, but few others ever seem to be able to see and anticipate their needs. They stubbornly determine that they will not lower themselves to asking to have their needs met, falsely believing that everyone is as capable of seeing and addressing the needs of others as they are.

If you see yourself in this description, understand that Relaters make up only thirty-eight percent of the population. That means, under ideal circumstances, you have just slightly better than one chance in three of having someone with whom you relate see and anticipate your needs. None of the other temperaments are so inclined. The actual truth though, is that your odds are considerably worse than that, because Relaters tend to attract types other than Relaters to themselves. They often find themselves surrounded by Entertainers who love to talk, because Relaters are good listeners, or by Commanders who love to control, because Relaters are easily controlled. So, if you expect there to come a day when those people with whom you associate will just magically begin to see and fulfill your needs without your asking, think again.

The Relater's greatest flaws are being too indecisive and too secretive about their wants and needs. They can also be stubborn when they feel put upon. Negative Relaters are often too needy, wanting and expecting other people to fill their needs and order their lives for them. They take little to no responsibility for themselves, and can become quite a burden on the caretaker.

Negative Relaters prefer watching to doing, in almost every area of their lives, so they can seem quite lazy, undirected and uninspired. They seem to have no ambition and no drive, so others are constantly having to push them to get anything done. When they are pushed, however, they just dig their heels in, and become all the more stubborn and difficult. Motivating this type of Relater can be a very big challenge.

To Be an Effective Relater

1. The best thing you can do for yourself is to learn to be more outspoken. Learn to ask for what you want. Realize that your own wants and needs are just as important as those of others, and that you have a right to have your own wants and needs fulfilled, at least part of the time. Realize that people are not mind readers and that, in order to get your needs met, you will have to let others know what they are.

2. Being flexible and agreeable is wonderful and other people absolutely love those attributes in the Relater. But, when they are so extreme as to cause personal discomfort, prevent you from getting your needs met, and cause other people to get angry with you for never stating your position or speaking your mind, those potentially delightful traits have become a problem for you and others. Realize that the best way to have good, strong relationships is through a process of give and take. Learn to receive as well as to give. Set some personal boundaries and learn to protect them from those who would violate them.

3. Realize that it's okay to say "no." Learn to refuse unreasonable requests gently but firmly. It will be easier to say no to someone and maintain good will (which is very important to you) if you suggest alternatives to the request. If, for example, someone asks you to watch their dog for them while they are out of town, it would be easier to say "I would love to help you if I could, but I can't. Perhaps you could get Sandy to watch your dog. Or there is a very good kennel over on First Street." This says to the other

person, I want to help you with your problem, but I can't help you the way you suggested.

4.   Realize that if you always let others win, you will often lose, and soon you will have nothing left to give to yourself or anyone else. Learn to be more assertive. Let other people know what you think, how you feel, and what your position is on things that matter to you. Strive for win/win situations, where you get to win right along with those you care about.

5.   Refuse to put yourself out all the time, in order to give to those who demand too much of your time and energy. Learn to put yourself first occasionally. This won't be an easy thing for you to do initially, but it will get easier as you begin to see that a less wishy-washy position actually improves your relationships.

6.   It is vital that you learn to take an active part in the process of living. You don't need to get up on stage or run out on the playing field, but you do need to start calling more of your own shots. You need to learn to make decisions and to state your wants and needs.

7.   Use your assets of flexibility and patience to move you forward and help you to reach your own goals. You have the capacity to enlist the help of others too, so use it. You probably have a long list of people who you have done good things for over the years. It's likely these people would be delighted to assist you in reaching your goals. You'll be doing them a great favor by asking them for assistance. It's human nature to want to return kindnesses and, if you are a typical Relater, there are lots of people

waiting for you to let them know you need their help. Remember, you don't appear to need any help, so no one ever suspects you might need their assistance. Let them know, and you'll soon see how very valuable all the points you've accrued helping others can be.

Some Good Career Choices for Relaters

Relaters can be effective in any area where there is a climate of caring and mutual respect. They are great team players and prefer to work within groups that feel supportive. They prefer to do work that has some value to other people, and that provides structure and stability to themselves.

Some good choices are:
- Medical Technician
- Lab Technician
- Nurse
- Physical Therapist
- Massage Therapist
- Dentist
- Dental or Veterinary Assistant
- Psychologist
- Psychiatrist
- Social Worker
- Teacher
- Counselor
- Minister
- Religious Educator

- Customer Service Representative
- Computer Operator
- Surveyor
- Beautician
- Bank Teller
- Middle Manager
- Administrator
- Secretary
- Personnel Director
- Diplomat

Relater Overview

Tendencies
- Flexible
- Easygoing
- Amiable
- Helpful
- Caring
- Calm
- Thoughtful
- Indecisive
- Loyal
- Appears Gentle and Reserved

Needs
- Reassurance
- Guidance
- Flexibility
- Freedom from Conflict

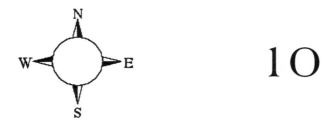

The Entertainer
(originally Sanguine)

━━━ ━ ━━ ━ ━━ ━ ━━ ━ ━━ ━ ━━ ━ ━━ ━ ━━ ━ ━━ ━ ━━ ━ ━━ ━ ━━

When Kimberly walks into a room, the entire room lights up! Her electric smile and sparkling eyes immediately attract you, and make you want to smile back. She is bubbly, optimistic, and playful, and her enthusiasm is contagious.

If Kimberly has any personal space requirements, I haven't seen them yet. She will walk right up to your face, beaming at you, and in that moment you become the most important person on earth to her. At least, that's how she makes you feel. She focuses all her attention on you, and starts asking you questions about yourself, your day, your work, your life, your kids, or just about anything else you might have going.

Of course, the questions are only conversation starters, and once you get caught up in her energy, she takes the conversational lead and runs with it, but ... what the heck! ... you feel so appreciated with all that attention focused on you momentarily, you don't really mind that you are just one of hundreds. You forget that all the attention doesn't really mean you are all that special ... everyone gets that kind of attention, at least for a little while. Even when Kimberly takes over and starts doing most of the talking, you are totally swept up. It's hard not to be. She can make the most mundane of subjects seem exciting with her dramatic flair and colorful stories.

Kimberly is dating my youngest son, Ron, who is an Organizer/Commander combination. He is reserved and serious most of the time. Though he loves adventure and challenge, he approaches even these with a sort of serious-ness. He is decisive and direct. He tells it like it is, and if you can't handle it ... Hey! toughen up! ... that's life! Most people see Ron that way, but not Kimberly. With her flair for adding color, Ron becomes bigger than life, a wonderful character out of some heroic novel, a knight in shining armor ready to rescue her at any moment. Certainly romance has something to do with Kimberly's view of Ron, but the added color and drama are clearly the hallmarks of her Entertainer nature.

General Entertainer Traits

The Entertainer, like the Commander, is a natural extrovert. They are outgoing, gregarious and sociable. Like Kimberly, Entertainers are dramatic and colorful. Their world is one big storybook filled with heroes to cheer, and villains to be hissed and booed. Whatever an Entertainer feels is displayed, with dramatic flair, for all the world to see. They seem to enjoy their emotions. They react imme-diately and powerfully to life's events. They seek emotional experiences and have little interest in the serious side of life.

Entertainers are good-natured, sentimental, romantic, passionate, and reactive. They can go from joy to anger to misery to resignation to despair and back to joy again, in the space of one afternoon. Although they are emotional and can be erratic at times, Entertainers don't stay angry long, and they don't hold a grudge. They don't expect others to hold grudges either.

When Kimberly gets upset with Ron, she lets him know it immediately. Sometimes she is too direct and blunt, and Ron's slow-to-release Organizer traits cause him to internalize the comment and let it simmer. Five minutes after the incident, Kimberly will come bouncing in, her usual happy self, look at Ron's forlorn face and ask, "Honey, what's wrong?" She is totally sincere about it too. Ron can't imagine how someone can be cold one minute and hot the next. It just isn't in his nature to turn his feelings off and on. Kimberly can't understand why Ron is letting "such a little thing" eat at him. To her the incident is over. She's already forgotten the whole thing, so why hasn't he?

Entertainers can change moods as easily as other people might change radio stations. Theirs is the only temperament that can do that, which means they often leave the other types wondering what is going on back at "A" long after the Entertainer has moved on to "X," "Y" and "Z."

Entertainers love people ... well, actually, they love to entertain people. They truly enjoy the social side of life and, even when negative nurturing has left them shy and fearful, as was my case, they still enjoy the social process vicariously. But rather than jumping in and becoming a part of things, as is the case for uninhibited Entertainers, the inhibited ones watch the process, long for it, and place themselves within it in their imaginations and dreams. This is true to some extent for the other types as well, because the Entertainer temperament is the one that is held up to the American culture as the social ideal by the media. All those ads you see where people are interacting easily and happily are representations of the Entertainer temperament. So, while the other three types may have some level of desire to interact this way because of our cultural nurturing, for the true Entertainer it goes beyond just a wish to be that way. For them it is a deep and incessant longing.

Entertainers love social gatherings and parties. That glowing, gregarious soul you see at parties, dancing and prancing around, entertaining the entire crowd, easily hugging half the guests, is either very drunk or is an Entertainer! (Possibly both!) Entertainers are likely to do whatever they feel has entertainment value; whatever will draw attention to themselves or other people to them. They enjoy the process of mixing and mingling. No one is a stranger for long around a true Entertainer. They can strike up a conversation anywhere, any time, and with just about anyone. And since attention is so important to Entertainers, they are usually very careful with grooming. They pay attention to how they look and act. They know that to get attention and gain acceptance, you have to make a good impression, and they are usually masters at it.

Their strengths are in the fact that they interact with people so well, are energetic and playful, spontaneous and adventurous. Entertainers are good on stage and can be very enchanting. They have a happy-go-lucky attitude and a childlike innocence that makes them fun to be around. Their tendency to act on impulse and go with the moment keeps life either interesting and exciting, or unpredictable and draining, depending on one's point of view.

Entertainers love to talk, but they are not especially good at listening. They tend to be thinking about the next thing they will say, when they are supposed to be listening, so a great deal of information slips right past them. They come across as scattered and "clueless" much of the time as a result of this tendency. Actually, Entertainers are just as intelligent as any of the other temperaments, but their myriad interests and their desire to take it all in at once can make them appear scattered at times.

Entertainers want to experience everything. Everything that life has to offer is worthy of their attention and it's just too hard to ignore all that stuff to concentrate on just one thing for long. They usually have several projects going simultaneously, because they love starting things. Beginnings are exciting to Entertainers, so they usually start things in a very enthusiastic way, but quickly get bored and move on to something else. Projects lose their flavor quickly for Entertainers, and they often find it difficult to stick with one until it's completed.

The scattered thinking tends to make Entertainers somewhat forgetful, too. They forget names, dates, appointments, and a host of other things. They also lack a good sense of direction, and tend to get lost fairly regularly. They don't just lose their way though; they tend to lose things as well, lots of things. Their inattention to detail is the main cause for this. Most people lose little things like car keys occasionally, but it is not uncommon for an Entertainer to lose their entire car! This generally occurs because, as they are parking their car, they are thinking about why they are there, what they are going to do, who they are going to meet, etc. They are not thinking about something as mundane as parking the car, so they forget to notice the surrounding details that would lead them back to their parking spot. They just get out of their car and bounce off to do whatever it is they are there to do. Not until it's time to return to the car, do they even remotely realize that they didn't notice where they parked and now have no idea where the car might be!

While Entertainers have difficulty remembering details, they have an excellent memory for colors, shapes, faces, etc. This fact can be used to compensate for the lack of memory for other kinds of details by associating colors, shapes or other visuals with the less interesting details that need to be remembered.

Entertainers are sometimes described by the more staid types as scattered or fickle, but even the staid folks can't help but be charmed by Entertainers. To them the whole world is a stage and they are excellent at playing their parts!

Some Negative Traits to Watch For

All Entertainers love to talk and like attention, but the negative types tend to gossip, repeat stories over and over (to the same people) and neglect to pay enough attention to other people (who often send out all kinds of non-verbal clues to indicate that the Entertainer is boring them to death, and which negative Entertainers usually ignore). They are uncomfortable when they are not the center of attention, and will do almost anything to get noticed. They laugh too loud, talk too loud, tease, interrupt — whatever it takes.

Negative Entertainers are overly sensitive. They can become so involved in their own emotional dramas that they seem completely unaware of the people and circumstances around them. They over-dramatize and exaggerate their lives so much that others can never take them seriously — an upset stomach equals cancer, a disapproving glance equals attack with intent to kill, a fender bender equals a totaled car, ten pounds overweight equals a ton. Everything is so big and overwhelming to a negative Entertainer.

Like little children, negative Entertainers want immediate gratification of all their needs. If they don't get it, they get tearful or angry. They need constant reassurance and praise, yet when they are praised, they don't believe it. They see nothing praiseworthy in themselves, so any praise others give them must be a mistake. They are unhappy people who believe that misery loves company, so they make sure they spread it around.

To Be an Effective Entertainer

1. Learn to be more observant. Pay attention to the things other people say, both verbally and non-verbally. Watch their expressions. Get to know other people as much as you want them to know you. There is much more to life than just being interesting and entertaining.

2. Entertainers tend to be somewhat disorganized. They have very loose "filing systems" and a rather casual approach to orderliness, which can drive the more organized types crazy. The Entertainer's inattention to detail and their need to do things in a spontaneous way are the main causes of their disorganization. They tend to be right-brain thinkers who are very visual, and because of their need to be able to see everything, they tend to keep things out, where they can be seen, rather than stored away. Out of sight really is out of mind for the Entertainer. Use your creativity to come up with a filing system you can live with. Color-coded systems and lots of Post-it Notes are helpful ways to get more organized. Use the Post-it Notes to remind you to take

things from a file or other storage place when it's time to work on it.

3. Entertainers are procrastinators. There are so many exciting things to do in the world that it's easy to put off the less interesting things, like balancing the checkbook, paying the bills, making dental appointments, cleaning house, organizing your desk, etc. Some of these things can be delegated, if you happen to be in a position to do that, but many must be done personally. Keep a daily schedule and schedule the less exciting things where you can do them fairly early in your day. That way they will be out of the way and you can spend the rest of the day doing things you enjoy more.

4. If you tend to lose things (including yourself), learn to pay more attention to your surroundings. Connect colors, shapes and images to parking places, storage places, filing systems, etc. This takes conscious effort at first, but with time it becomes more natural. You will be amazed at how much less frustrating your life can be when you take the time to pay attention to what you are doing and where you are going, and to create a system that brings greater order into your life.

5. Work on being a better listener. You like to talk and can forget to listen at times. When you don't listen, people can tell you things that are important for you to hear and you will miss them. If people often tell you they told you something that you don't remember being told, the problem is probably not your memory as much as it is your listening skills. You may want to take a class on effective listening, then put what you learn to use.

6.   You tend to ignore things you find unpleasant or annoying, rather than dealing with them. Unfortunately some things keep hanging around, getting bigger and meaner, until we deal with them. Learn to deal with unpleasant situations before they get out of hand. It's better to feel anxious and uncomfortable for a little while, in order to deal with a situation early, than to wait until it's a major production. Unpleasant things seldom go away of their own accord and when they start piling up, you can become completely overwhelmed. Early attention to problems will render far better outcomes for you.

Some Good Career Choices for Entertainers

Entertainers want to be around people. They want a lot of flexibility, latitude and room for spontaneity. They are great motivators and inspirers, who can charm people into almost anything. Their greatest asset to a company is in their ability to deal with people effectively.

Some good choices are:
- Public Relations
- Sales
- Journalist
- Playwright
- Reporter
- Marketing Consultant
- Creative Director
- Personal Consultant
- Character Actor

- Entertainer
- Cartoonist
- Interior Decorator
- Art/Drama Teacher
- Special Education Teacher
- Schoolteacher
- Pastoral Counselor
- Psychologist
- Social Scientist
- Human Resources Manager
- Conference/Party Planner

Entertainer Overview

Tendencies
- Sociable
- Colorful
- Energetic
- Talkative
- Loves Attention
- Entertaining
- Good Communicator
- Dramatic
- Emotional
- Enjoys and Seeks Out Group Activities
- Appears Playful and Enthusiastic

Needs
- Friendship
- Recognition/Attention
- Freedom from Constraints and Detail

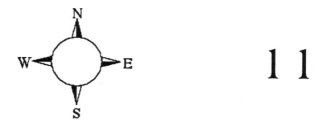

Combination Profiles

Your dominant temperament alters your secondary temperament, like chocolate syrup alters milk. The basic product is still there and still has all its properties intact, but it looks and tastes different than the unflavored variety. Your secondary traits add flavor and color to your dominant ones in the same manner. The variation can be very subtle or it can be quite dramatic, depending on how much "flavoring" is added by the secondary trait. If the strength of the secondary temperament is almost equal to the dominant one, you have lots of flavoring, and the traits inherent to your secondary temperament may be almost equal those of the dominant one. If the dominant trait is a lot higher than the secondary, you have just a hint of flavor added, and the traits of your dominant temperament are the most utilized. If your dominant temperament is more than seventy-five percent higher than your secondary, you are a true type, and you have no "flavoring" to speak of.

To see how the dominant and secondary traits function together, find your particular combination on the following pages and read the description. Begin with your own combination, as you did in the temperaments section, then go back later to familiarize yourself with the other combinations.

The Commander/Entertainer Combination

This combination is a very dynamic one. Those within this combination are highly inventive, energetic and enthusiastic. They enjoy people, but prefer to be in a leadership position for the most part. This type is good at handling large groups of people. They are more fun-loving than a pure Commander type, but less so than a pure Entertainer. They enjoy a large variety of activities and love the processes of dreaming, scheming and developing their ideas. However, once developed, they want to move on to the next challenge and (unless there is constant stimulation) have some difficulty sticking to any one thing for long. Anything repetitive or too easily accomplished quickly loses its appeal.

This combination loves a challenge and thrives on intellectual stimulation. They prefer to learn by challenging themselves and testing their limits. Because of this, they are constantly seeking new ideas and new adventures. They are risk takers who love competition (true entrepreneurial types). They prefer to work with grand projects and don't really care for detail. Details and routine frustrate this type as a rule, so whenever possible the details are left to others. However, when this type believes only they can produce the desired result, they are perfectly willing to handle the details themselves in order to achieve that result. They don't tend to place a lot of emphasis on being organized however, so things that require a lot of attention to detail and organization can become frustrating. These people are independent thinkers who prefer to do their own thing. They see relationships as opportunities for the growth and development of both parties and if this is not the result, they have little difficulty writing a relationship off.

A Commander/Entertainer combination is slightly more businesslike and success-focused than the Entertainer/Commander combination, which is more people-focused and leans more in the direction of the fun-loving entertainer.

Some famous people who present as Commander/Entertainers are Donald Trump and Bette Midler.

The Entertainer/Commander Combination

This type of individual is very extroverted, powerful and persuasive, in fact the most persuasive of all the combinations. They are natural leaders who are both capable and caring ... a nice combination of decisiveness and supportiveness. They also can be great motivators. They are imaginative, inspirational and dynamic. They are (or have the capacity to become) great communicators who enjoy center stage and revel in the limelight.

This combination truly loves people, but can be sensitive and easily wounded by them. They are smooth talkers who tend to lay out plans for themselves, as well as others, assuming that the others are in agreement with them and when they are not, the Entertainer/Commander tends to take it personally.

They are goal-oriented and fairly well organized, although their organizational style is not necessarily what an Organizer would call orderly. Their idea of organized is keeping things controllable. As with other Commander combinations, maintaining some level of control is important. This type makes excellent negotiators.

Some famous people who present as Entertainer/ Commanders are Ronald Reagan and Tom Cruise.

The Commander/Organizer Combination

The Commander/Organizer combination expresses as an individual who tends to be very serious about life. This combination is both driven and detailed. They can see the big picture and attend to the little details, so they are formi- dable business people as a rule. When Commander/ Organizers set their minds to accomplishing something, it gets accomplished one way or the other.

This combination isn't especially interested in social affairs. They would rather be accomplishing something they consider of value, something that will improve their standing in the world. This is a dynamic mix that usually presents itself as "serious energy." These are life's adminis- trators ... handing out directives, structuring, scheduling and ordering. They are serious about their goals, grounded, organized, exacting and capable. They are dependable and able to get the job done in a direct and practical way. They are quite powerful and can be a dominant force in a business setting, but in social settings they can become quite timid.

They prefer structured relationships and tend to have sharply defined roles for each one. For example, they have specific ideas as to how children should behave, and what a spouse, boss or friend should be like. They want to be in control in their relationships (it's that Commander thing again) and if they are, they can be quite pleasant. However, if someone tries to control them, they can get obstinate. This type tends to order people around, though they are not always aware they are doing this. Even children of this combination have that tendency. They respect firm resistance when it is justified, however, and tend to work toward an equitable compromise with those they perceive as strong and directed enough to work with.

This combination tends to be firm, directed and self-disciplined, sometimes to the point of stubborn. They are more extroverted and outwardly dynamic than the Organizer/Commander combination, which tends to be somewhat reserved, but in either direction this combination is a powerhouse with a mission.

Some famous people who present as Commander/ Organizers are Steven Spielberg, Ross Perot and Bill Gates.

The Organizer/Commander Combination

This combination, like the Commander/Organizer, can see the big picture complete with every detail, and can be extremely effective at planning and coordinating, but they tend to be less aggressive and somewhat more reserved in their approach. They have excellent organizational skills as a rule, and don't mind taking the lead in organized settings.

This type tends to be highly independent, and they can come across as distant, aloof and even argumentative at times. What they see as "friendly discussion," others see as arguing or hostility. This combination has definite ideas as to what (in their opinion) represents excellence, which they not only strive for personally, but also tend to insist on in others, making them appear somewhat opinionated and judgmental. They believe there is always room for improvement and actively seek ways to make things "better." They love goal-setting and "to do" lists, tend to be project-oriented and to finish what they start. They may try to control the activities and outcomes of others, but insist on having the freedom to explore alternatives, experiment, change and improve things themselves. They can become quite frustrated if too tightly curtailed or controlled, and will either become belligerent or will withdraw and become silent and obstinate. Their Organizer side makes them quite sensitive, and their Commander side compels them to seek success. Because of this, they often have great ideals and specific ideas as to what a perfect world should look like, and they are willing to expend great amounts of time and energy to convince others to see it their way. Properly channeled, their idealism can lead to some very valuable insights and important changes; unchanneled, it tends to lead only to disputes and hard feelings.

This combination can benefit greatly by learning to communicate their ideas with less gravity and more empathy, and to allow others the right to their own opinions. Those who have learned to do this tend to be highly respected and sought out for their wisdom, vision and ability to create excellence.

Some famous people who present as Organizer/ Commanders are Katharine Hepburn and Dustin Hoffman.

The Commander/Relater Combination

This combination is one of opposition. The Commander side of this combination is driven and extroverted, while the Relater side is laid-back and introverted. The Commander wants to accomplish and the Relater wants to take it easy. As you might imagine, this can be quite frustrating to this type of individual until he or she either learns to deal with the opposition, or eliminates it by moving toward the natural dominant trait.

This is a "to work or not to work" combination. Most of the people I have met with this combination handle the opposition in one of two ways: they either work like crazy when at work and when they get home, park themselves in an easy chair, kick back and refuse to budge; or they work like the devil for three or four days, maybe putting in fifty hours, then they sleep and laze around for three or four days.

Needless to say, the latter type has a terrible time trying to hold down a regular job and usually resorts to something entrepreneurial so they can work their own hours. Sometimes they work at several odd jobs to achieve that kind of flexibility. This combination can be very frustrating to others, who don't understand their unorthodox approach to life. They don't always understand it themselves.

How much time this opposition spends driving themselves compared to how much is spent avoiding work, depends on whether they are a Commander/Relater or a Relater/Commander. The Commander/Relater is more driven, of course.

This combination also has a curious mix of caring about the feelings of other people but not having the patience to deal with them for very long. They often become loners because they don't know how to handle this ambiguity. While people with this combination tend to be doers and problem-solvers, they can also be quite gregarious and entertaining at times. They are the ultimate realists with "do it now" attitudes when in work mode, and the ultimate dreamers with a *mañana* attitude when in relaxed mode. Commander/Relaters tend to function best in work mode, where they can be very action-oriented. They are doers who just wade into things and try to figure it out as they go. A sort of "if all else fails, read the instructions" type. They are driven and objective, while at the same time flexible, spontaneous and open to suggestions. They enjoy speculation so much that they can take a small suggestion and carry it all the way to the moon and back. These way out ideas often go nowhere though, because this combination, being the "wade-into-it" type, dislikes planning and preparation and tends not to do much of it.

Commander/Relaters tend to pursue practical things, and to confine their activities and learning to what is immediately useful and relevant. They dislike established norms, rules, procedures, and requirements and, in this sense, they can be real rebels, either actively or passively resisting authority figures. They do whatever they do for its perceived value rather than because they think they should or ought to do it. They are competitive, restless, realistic and will try just about anything once.

Famous people with oppositions are hard to find, because they don't often present the opposition to the world. Any people listed in the opposition combinations are listed only for how they appear. They may not, in fact, have this opposition.

Some famous people who appear to be Commander/Relater combinations are Willie Nelson and kd lang.

The Relater/Commander Combination

This combination is the typical absent-minded professor type. They are fully aware of what is, but they also can see so many possibilities. This combination loves to look at what already exists and then to imagine all the ways it might be better. Of course, they don't always actually get around to making it better, but when they do, they usually know what to do. They spend a great deal of time thinking things through, but as little time as possible actually doing. They are constantly looking for the easiest way to get things done, so they won't have to work too hard. They can seem indecisive at times, because they are always waiting for completion in what they see as an eternally growing and changing amount of data. They are never quite sure that today's decision will be the best decision and they want to leave their options open in case a last minute improvement appears.

They see this type of holding back as necessary to ensure competency or flawless outcomes (which they strive for). Once they are convinced that a course of action is a good one, however, the Commander part kicks in and they can be quite driven and directed until that project is completed. In general Relater/Commanders love to think, expand, reflect, clarify and then re-think, but they may lose interest at the point of actually doing. They are great at brainstorming ideas, but when it comes to carrying the ideas to completion, this combination would rather let someone else do that. They apply a problem-solving approach to almost everything — their work, their relationships, and even life itself. They prefer work that requires intellectual stimulation and very little, if any, manual labor. Though they will tolerate manual labor, they never enjoy it. Work that is predominantly a mental challenge tends to hold their interest best, and when interested, they can be infinitely patient in finding solutions and solving problems.

Famous people with oppositions are hard to find, because they don't often present the opposition to the world. So, any people listed in the opposition combinations are listed only for how they appear. They may not, in fact have this opposition.

Some famous people who appear to be Relater/Commander combinations are Albert Einstein and Benjamin Franklin.

The Entertainer/Organizer Combination

This is another opposition. In this one the question is "to play or not to play." The Entertainer part of this combination wants to enjoy people, to play, to enjoy life, but the Organizer part wants to be serious, to avoid crowds, to stay ordered and directed. Of the two oppositions, this one seems to create the most difficulties. Those I have encountered with this opposition tend to be very confused about their wants and needs. That's because their wants and needs are confusion personified. One part of this opposition says, "Play, have fun, enjoy life, get to know people, be the center of attention, life is a party! Enjoy it!" The other part says, "Don't even think about it. Life is serious. Work hard, keep your nose to the grindstone, take care of business, never make a spectacle of yourself! Be calm and conservative. Don't you dare act up and draw attention to yourself!"

Unlike the Commander/Relater opposition, this type doesn't usually manage to deal with their opposition very well. Those with this opposition tell me they will go through periods of extreme orderliness when they clean and organize everything, and then do a flip-flop and go through a period of what they call slovenliness. Then they get fed up with the chaos and flip-flop back to the orderly mode. The orderly/sloppy see-saw doesn't create as many problems as the "be serious/go play" see-saw, however.

Those who have learned to handle this opposition do so by finding friends or family members they feel free to be playful with and letting their playful sides go in this "safe" environment. They let the serious side reign the rest of the time. The Entertainer/Organizer is not as prone to seriousness as is the Organizer/Entertainer, but both combinations have difficulty with this opposition.

The Entertainer/Organizer can in fact be a wonderful host or hostess. They are open, friendly and attentive to details. They are gracious and effective in dealing with people. They tend to be meticulous and well-groomed and to keep their surroundings neat and orderly, but they are not perfectionistic like a true Organizer can be, so their surroundings seem more relaxed and comfortable to be in. But, they are not as gregarious as true Entertainers, and often prefer to entertain friends in their home rather than to go out to parties and large gatherings.

This combination has definite ideas as to what "appropriate" behavior is, and they tend to try to maintain that behavior in both self and others. They tend to be strict but affectionate disciplinarians. They prefer to run their lives according to some kind of self-arrived-at schedule, and resent having that schedule interrupted.

Those who lean in the direction of negative have a tendency to be somewhat critical of others, expressing lots of "shoulds" and "ought-tos," while at the same time preferring to sweep their own problems and shortcomings under the rug.

In general, this combination can be a delight to be around as long as they are in a secure (to them) setting.

Famous people with oppositions are hard to find, because they don't often present the opposition to the world. So, any people listed in the opposition combinations are listed only for how they appear. They may not, in fact have this opposition.

Some famous people who appear to be Entertainer/Organizer combinations are Jeff Bridges and Farrah Fawcett.

The Organizer/Entertainer Combination

This combination is more reserved than the Entertainer/Organizer combination, and can seem somewhat aloof at times. They are cautious socially, but tend to be adventurous and to enjoy daredevil kinds of things otherwise.

The opposition that exists within this combination results in an individual who is sometimes quiet and reserved, and sometimes playful; sometimes structured and sometimes spontaneous; sometimes fun, open and agreeable, and sometimes difficult, detached and hard to reach. Needless to say, this can keep others quite confused.

This combination tends to be skilled at working with their hands and tends to prefer working with ideas and things, rather than directly with people. They are highly observant, which makes them capable of understanding complex tasks without needing specific instructions. They would rather explore their options and discover new methods than to follow laid out procedures or directions. They can work with great precision and accuracy in areas that interest them, and tend to put off or avoid areas that don't. Interestingly, this can be a devil-may-care combination, with the Entertainer's adventurous side seeking thrills, and the Organizer's precision, working out ways to "safely" experience them. Because of this, individuals of this type are sometimes prone to living on the edge and putting themselves at risk.

Famous people with oppositions are hard to find, because they don't often present the opposition to the world. So, any people listed in the opposition combinations are listed only for how they appear. They may not, in fact have this opposition.

Some famous people who appear to be Organizer/Entertainer combinations are Burt Reynolds, Evel Knievel and Houdini.

The Entertainer/Relater Combination

This combination is a people combination. People are key to their happiness. This type both loves to entertain and to be entertained. They are talkers who are also willing to listen. They make great friends, counselors, customer service people or just about anything that involves dealing with people in a non-confrontational way. They are gregarious, outgoing and playful. They tend to be quite spontaneous, living for the moment, with a "play now/pay later" attitude. This combination tends to think in terms of immediate rewards and can find themselves in a pickle occasionally. They are usually not planners and tend to have a low tolerance for routines and procedures. Their live-and-let-live attitude makes them generally very tolerant of other people, and a delight to have as a friend.

This combination detests disagreement and any sort of conflict, and will work very hard to maintain harmony.

They tend to accentuate the positive and eliminate or diminish the negative in their friends and family, and within relationships. However, where their personal selves and life in general are concerned, this combination tends to be a worrier, usually assuming the worst. They are sometimes seen as "spacey," "flighty," or hyperactive, occasionally to the point of wearing others out.

They tend to be activity-oriented and like to juggle many things (and people) at once. Their tendency to be spontaneous and unmindful of consequences is often apparent in their abrupt, outspoken communication style. This combination sometimes seems to lack direction. They start far more than they finish and move quickly from one interest to another. They are easily frustrated by routine and restrictions, and tend not to have a very good sense of time or direction.

They enjoy surprises, the unknown and the unexpected, seeing these as the spice of life. This type's approach to life is one of easy playfulness. Life is not serious to them. They always seem to manage to find the rainbow behind the clouds. If things are not going well, they simply resign themselves to the circumstances and wait optimistically for better times, which they are sure will arrive eventually and, eventually, they always do.

Some famous people who present as Entertainer/Relater combinations are Meryl Streep, Daryl Hannah and Brad Pitt.

The Relater/Entertainer Combination

The Relater/Entertainer combination is warm, thoughtful and generous with their time. Their idea of fulfillment is in serving others in some noble way. They are generally easygoing, congenial, gentle and passive. They are givers who seldom, if ever, ask for anything in return. Yet, they expect that others will return their kindnesses, and when they fail to do so, Relater/Entertainers can become quite obstinate and hurt, feeling they are being taken advantage of or abused.

They tend to have very strict personal codes of ethics, which they neither share with nor impose on others. Because they tend not to talk about themselves or their wants and needs much, they can appear as somewhat secretive and unpredictable. They resist labels and stereotypes, and prefer to keep people guessing. They insist on self-identity, self-knowledge and, insofar as is possible, self-reliance. They have an open-ended approach to life (nothing is really final) and people are allowed to change their minds at the drop of a hat. And, of course, this type reserves that right for themselves as well. This combination is a very sensitive type whose feelings run deep, yet they seldom share their feelings with others. They have a gentle, easygoing exterior, but a compulsive, often stressful interior. The stress is often a result of trying to please all the people all the time and finding that to be an impossible task.

This type prefers to work with people in a teaching/counseling role rather than as a leader. When around people they tend to prefer to be a part of the team or group. They also enjoy time alone. Because Relater/Entertainers are so agreeable to be around, people very much enjoy their company. They are both poised and effervescent, which is a very attractive combination in a personality. These are people who can keep a gathering interesting and down-to-earth at the same time.

Some famous people who present as Relater/Entertainer combinations are Amy Irving and Cheryl Ladd.

The Organizer/Relater Combination

This combination tends to be serious in a gentle sort of way. They are more inclined to reach out to others and to allow others to get close to them than the true Organizer, but not as much so as the true Relater. This combination tends to be better at helping others find solutions to their problems than either of the true types. That's because they are not only empathetic and good at listening, they also have a knack for sorting out the details. This type tends to be methodical and ploddingly consistent. They may not get things done with the speed or energy of the Commander or the Commander/Entertainer, but they generally arrive in better shape and with greater reserves of energy over the long haul. They are the tortoises of "The Tortoise and the Hare" stories.

Besides their ability to help others and to get things accomplished in their own time, this combination seems to have a quiet resignation to life. They are sure that if they remain persistent and purposeful in their dealings, everything will eventually work out. They are steady workers, and it's their steady pace, their consistency and their genuine concern for achieving the best for all concerned that enables them to excel on a rather regular basis. Excellence is very much within the grasp of this temperament combination.

They can be gentle and compassionate, are good at working with and within groups, and tend to be quite good at reading other people. This combination is usually quiet and reserved but can be playful in a group where they feel safe and comfortable. Their thoughts and opinions are not easily expressed and must be drawn out by others. They tend to be steady, dependable, imaginative, helpful, sensitive, idealistic, quiet and introspective. They dislike conflict and work so hard at maintaining harmony that their efforts can create the very tension they are trying to avoid.

Some famous people who present as Organizer/ Relater combinations are Susan Sarandon, Sean Penn and Jon Voight.

The Relater/Organizer Combination

This combination prefers working behind the scenes or as a part of a group. They are quick, easygoing, adaptable, orderly, and willing to work with details. They tend to be service-oriented, empathetic listeners who are always willing to lend a shoulder to cry on. As with the other Relater combinations, they tend not to express their wants, needs and feelings easily.

Their high sense of commitment and feelings of obligation make them easily taken advantage of by those so inclined. This type has a very strong sense of duty and a need to obey "the rules" (whatever they perceive these to be). They have a strong work ethic which requires them to work first and play only when the work is done. They are neat and tidy, and tend to need a certain degree of order.

This combination is extremely loyal to those they care about. Males of this type are sometimes prone to outbursts of anger, insensitivity and other forms of extreme behavior in an effort to "prove" their masculinity, but at the core of both the males and females of this combination is a genuinely sensitive and caring soul.

Some famous people who present as Relater/ Organizer combinations are Nancy Reagan and Nicholas Cage.

Relating to the Other Temperaments

We usually have the most difficulty relating to our opposite type, which is unfortunate, because there is almost always something of value we can learn from them. Once we realize that no one type is right or wrong, we can better accept and relate to one another, and we can utilize one another's assets more readily. Each type is *different* to be sure, but differences are actually good. They keep life interesting and provide unique and specific benefits to the whole of mankind. For example:

- Commanders provide leadership, enterprise and achievement drive.
- Organizers provide order, structure and artistic beauty.
- Relaters provide compassion, gentleness and warmth.
- Entertainers provide excitement, playfulness and color.

When you can appreciate each of the types just the way they are, your relationships will improve a thousand times over. You will be amazed at how really wonderful most people are when approached in an accepting way.

The reason most people find relating to their opposite types difficult is because opposites often don't understand one another. You can improve your relationships with your opposite type by discovering and learning to appreciate what each of you has to offer the other. Greater understanding may not make your relationships perfect, but it sure will help.

Commanders and Relaters

The energy, enthusiasm and drive of the Commander is overpowering and mystifying to the quiet, easygoing Relater. Relaters think Commanders are rushing headlong into an early grave. What they don't understand is that Commanders actually adore their work and often consider leisure time a waste.

Relaters can't imagine life without leisure, and Commanders can't imagine how Relaters can be so unmotivated as to be content to "sit around doing nothing." Commanders think Relaters are listless, lazy, directionless, and going nowhere fast. They find it very hard to understand why Relaters aren't more driven. They see Relaters as too indecisive and wishy-washy. Relaters find Commanders too aggressive, overpowering and intimidating.

A business owner who attended one of my workshops was a very strong Commander, and as I was describing Relater types, he spoke up. "Those," he said, "are my problem at work. How do you motivate those guys?" This man happened to be surrounded by Relaters, and one of them muttered, half under his breath, "Well, it would probably help if he didn't approach them like that!"

I seized upon the opportunity. Here were four Relaters, one on each side of the Commander and two in front, who could teach the Commander something far better than I could. So I enlisted the help of all four Relaters and asked them to express their feelings to the Commander. And did they express their feelings! They had apparently been waiting all their lives for the opportunity to tell a Commander what they thought of him, and here was their chance. They did the Relater teamwork thing and, drawing on each other's ire, they lit into him.

The Commander was completely taken aback. He had no idea that his powerful demeanor and tough approach were so intimidating to Relaters, and said so. His surprise and amazement were very apparent to everyone in the room. He told the Relaters he had no idea he had been intimidating his people, or anyone for that matter, and that he would never do such a thing on purpose. I had heard this same sentiment from other amazed Commanders before and sanctioned the truth of what this Commander was telling them, as did all the other Commanders in the room.

The Relaters learned something that night too. They learned that sometimes people behave in ways that they consider perfectly natural, without intending harm. They also learned they could speak up to Commanders and would, perhaps, get a positive response, rather than the negative response they had previously imagined, feared and dreaded. As a result of the open, honest communication they had shared that night, everyone left the workshop with a better understanding of, and appreciation for, one another.

Commanders and Relaters can each offer the other balance, when they work in harmony with one another. Relaters can help Commanders to slow down a little and learn to enjoy leisure. Leisure for its own sake is good for the body and the soul, and Relaters can help Commanders discover this. Commanders, on the other hand, can motivate Relaters to be more decisive and to accomplish greater things. They can help them to stay directed and productive. Commanders can help Relaters succeed in business and Relaters can help Commanders succeed in maintaining their health and equilibrium.

Entertainers and Organizers

Entertainers, being outgoing, somewhat scattered and quite relaxed in the area of orderliness, can drive precise, meticulous, structured Organizers right up a wall. Organizers simply can't understand how someone can be so disoriented, disorganized, scattered and flippant. They think Entertainers are too flamboyant, too frivolous, too talkative, too absent-minded, too impatient and way too undisciplined. Their strongest urges when around Entertainers are to either "fix" them or file them away so they are never seen or heard from again. Organizers think everything should have a "file," a place for everything and everything in its place. The only problem is, they aren't sure what the "place" for Entertainers is.

Entertainers can't tolerate all the detail Organizers give in answering "simple" questions. They find Organizers too serious, too boring, too detailed, too ordered, and way too controlled for their own (or anybody else's) good. They are no fun! They don't know how to play! Organizers are "wet blankets" out to spoil everyone's fun, according to Entertainers.

Entertainers and Organizers are quite different souls to be sure, but each has something very valuable to offer the other. Organizers are great at taking care of all the details that Entertainers never manage to get around to handling. They are also helpful in finishing or urging Entertainers to finish all the projects they tend to start, but not finish. Entertainers can lead Organizers into a level of playfulness that they can thoroughly enjoy, but which Organizers would not be likely to partake in without the lead of the Entertainer.

Entertainers never seem to manage to get themselves completely organized without the help of an Organizer, and

Organizers never quite manage to let their hair down and be a kid again, without the Entertainer. It isn't uncommon for me to suggest some adventure to my Organizer-Relater husband, George, and have him go along with it for my sake, only to discover he enjoyed it as much or more than I did. I help him to be more playful, but he keeps my life orderly, organized and better directed. It's a wonderful exchange for both of us!

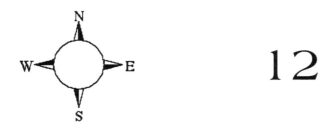

Your Nurture —
Understanding
External Influences

Susan, my mother-in-law, is ninety-five years old. Her mother, she recalls, was a wonderful cook who regularly made scrumptious desserts. Susan often watched her mother make these marvelous morsels, but she seldom got to eat them. Her mother, it seems, had a rule that whenever there were guests in the house, the guests got dessert first. If there was any left over, the children got some. The problem was, they often had guests and seldom had any dessert left over. So Susan watched, waited, hoped, and longed to get her share, but she was, more often than not, left wanting.

At some point in her young life, she decided that if she ever got in a position to be able to provide herself with desserts, she would have all she wanted. Now, ninety-plus years later, she is still keeping that vow — still functioning on that old program that says, "Dessert equals specialness." Not one day goes by that she doesn't have something sweet, and she thinks she must have it. You don't dare put dessert down in front of her before she has eaten some of her meal, because the minute she sees it, the meal is abandoned and the dessert gets devoured. That is how powerful and long-lasting the things that influence our lives externally can be.

Nature is a powerful force and it tries very hard to maintain a dominant position, but time and time again I encounter people who have been affected by so many external forces that they don't even know what their nature is now. Many people wear dark, heavy masks that effectively disguise and suppress their true nature, just as I once did.

The many influences we have been subjected to since birth are what weave the second part of our overall "personality." Some of those external factors are positive ones that actually enhance our nature, polishing it to a brilliant shine. The negative ones, however, obscure natural tendencies and prevent us from growing into all we have the capacity to become. Negative influencers are like a thick, heavy mud that buries the treasures we were born with, and sometimes prevents us from ever becoming aware of them.

In this chapter we are going to look at how those external factors have affected your image of yourself and your way of interacting with the world, by comparing your temperamental traits to your preferences.

Preferences, while usually fairly constant, are certainly subject to change. These changes can and do result from a number of factors. Sometimes it's a result of our gaining independence from our parents. Sometimes it's because something important occurs in our lives to make us re-examine ourselves — a death, a birth, a new awareness.

If your early influences were negative, they may have required you to adopt a set of preferences other than those you would have adopted by nature. You adopted those preferences to minimize the pain and discomfort you encountered within the context of your family, educational and/or social environments.

Negative conditioning, or what I sometimes refer to as "negative nurturing," is any influence exerted upon an individual by outside forces which served to alter or control the individual in ways that were not beneficial to their growth and development. These negative influences can be as subtle as manipulating through excess shows of concern or through "teaching," or as blatant as outright abuse. Whatever form they take though, if our nature is in conflict with our nurturing, as is often the case with negatively nurtured individuals, we grow up feeling lost, confused, and without any real sense of who or what we really are.

Quite often, as we grow older and begin to move farther and farther away from the direct influence of our parents, guardians or other significant people, our nature begins to exert more influence on us than the early nurturing is now exerting. When that occurs, we tend to begin moving toward our true nature, and to feel ourselves being pulled in different directions than those we have become accustomed to. The discomfort of this tugging causes us to respond in one of three ways: (1) we either resist the changes and deal with the discomfort, because we haven't managed to let go of the early programming yet; (2) we cautiously allow change to occur gradually and very slowly; or (3) we make broad, sweeping changes that sometimes require us to move rapidly toward previously unused and undeveloped preferences.

The latter approach is often seen by others as rebellion (if we're still young) or the "middle-age-crazies" if we happen to be older.

We may also change our preferences as a result of value shifts, which occur when something happens in our life that causes us to step back and question things we once took for granted. Things such as divorce, loss of a loved one, loss of a job, or even reading a book that touches us, can cause us to re-evaluate our lives and question our old belief systems. Value shifts cause us to look at life (or at least parts of it) differently and, as a result, to approach certain aspects of our lives in new and different ways.

Workshop participants tell me quite often that they have changed considerably since they were children. They often believe that the changes they have observed mean that their temperaments have changed over the years. They have not. Generally, any changes we experience over the years occur as a result of changing our way of acting and inter-acting, or as a result of altering our preferences, belief systems, or one or more of our early values in an effort to adjust to our surroundings. Our basic temperaments can be suppressed, but they never change.

Although we certainly have the capacity to act in any way we choose, certain actions, interactions and behaviors are more difficult for us than others.

Social mingling will never be entirely comfortable for an introvert, for example. An extrovert would never be entirely comfortable in a job that kept him isolated. Someone who was born to be a talker finds it very difficult to sit quietly where there is a conversation going on, while a natural listener is perfectly happy to do so.

Not all people are aware of their nature. Many people have been functioning in an uncomfortable mode for so long that they think that's the way life feels, as I once did. They don't know that the discomfort they feel is the result of early influences that continue to pull them in opposing directions.

Our nature usually asserts itself only when early influences have caused us to adjust in ways that didn't enhance our natural capabilities. We don't, for example, usually have any problem with training that enables us to function well within society. Good grooming, politeness, cleanliness and other such training serves us, enhances us. We don't want to undo those kinds of things.

But there are areas of early training that don't enhance us, they hold us back. Our families, cookie-cutter school systems and societal norms may have required adjustments from us that were not ultimately beneficial. Family dynamics may crush a child's natural boldness by teaching him that he must be compliant, must never ask questions or argue. Cookie-cutter school systems teach talkative little extroverts that talking is bad. Societal norms teach us that boys act one way and girls another.

When you observe yourself changing and behaving differently as you get older and more mature, usually it's because your nature is trying to step in and replace the conditioning that pulled you off track when you were a child.

The best way to determine whether or not you are moving through life in accordance with your nature is to look at your level of comfort and happiness in the various areas of your life. In areas where you are happy and content, you are functioning in accordance with your nature. In areas where you experience consistent discomfort, you are most likely functioning contrary to your nature.

The only exception would be when you are learning a new skill and don't yet feel proficient at it. It isn't uncommon to feel uncomfortable as we move into new areas or begin to try new things, but I am not referring to new experiences here. I am referring to areas of your life that are not new to you, but that are still not pleasant or enjoyable.

Say, for example, that you are a personnel director for a large corporation and you love your job. What you like most about it is the interaction with all the employees. You like interviewing new job applicants, you enjoy helping current employees with their needs, and you like the fact you are a highly visible person in your company.

At home, however, you have a spouse who is somewhat reclusive and doesn't really care to go out or visit other people very much, so you are quite isolated once you get home. The spouse is good to you, in general, but there is this nagging need to break free. You just don't understand it. There is no problem you can put your finger on, and you feel a little guilty for being dissatisfied.

Your nature, in such instances, is trying to tell you something. In this instance, you could pinpoint your need for social stimulation if you knew your temperament well enough. You would then realize that you don't need to change spouses, you just need to find ways to have more social interactions outside of work, with or without your spouse accompanying you.

By knowing *where* you are off track, you can make adjustments more easily. That's the value of taking both profiles and comparing the results of your preferences profile to those of your temperaments profile. The comparison enables you to determine how closely your current way of relating to your world matches your self-perception of your nature. If the two don't match, you will know why and, quite often, you'll also know what to do about it.

Attitudes and Functions

Attitudes describe how we view and relate to other people, events and the world in general. They also describe how we prefer to receive and use energy and to be stimulated.

The thinking and feeling functions describe how we prefer to make decisions. The thinking function makes decisions using cognitive skills, comparing and relating external facts or observations. The feeling function utilizes internal perceptions, and makes decisions based on the value of the experience or on how the experience feels, rather than on the specifics of it.

The sensation and intuition set of functions describes the way we prefer to gather data and information, and to become aware of things. Sensation uses external stimuli to become aware of things through the use of color, shape, arrangement and facts, while the intuition becomes aware of things internally. It sees the same things and events as sensation, but rather than looking directly at the facts, intuition sees what is going on behind or beneath the actual facts. Sensation looks at the what of an event, where the intuition looks at the why and how of it.

To determine your particular preferential mix, complete the Preferences Profile questions on the following pages. This is not an in-depth profile, such as you would gain by taking the entire *C.O.R.E. Multi-Dimensional Awareness Profile* (C.O.R.E. MAP), but it is sufficient to get you started.

C.O.R.E. Multi-dimensional Awareness Profile
Part 2 — Preferences

Instructions

Read the sets of statements on the following pages and choose the statement in each pair that best suits you.

In some instances, *both* statements will apply to some extent, but one will always be more applicable than the other. Choose the one that describes you best overall. Choose only *one* from each set.

The fact that you are choosing one over the other does not mean you would *always* choose that one over the other, only that you tend to choose that particular option *most often*.

Again, be honest with yourself. There is no value to you in a false profile. Complete all three sections.

Section 1

When relating to others and the world at large, I tend to:

1 A. _____ Project my energy outward in an outgoing, easily visible way.

1 B. _____ Keep my energy controlled in a fairly reserved way.

2 A. _____ Move toward activity and action.

2 B. _____ Stick to ideas and thoughts.

3 A. _____ Interact easily — I don't mind crowds and noise.

3 B. _____ *Avoid* crowds and enjoy solitude.

4 A. _____   Express myself and expect others to do the same.

4 B. _____   Keep my thoughts to myself.

5 A. _____   Feel lonely or irritable fairly soon after being isolated from activity.

5 B. _____   Feel agitated and irritable fairly soon after being around a lot of activity.

6 A. _____   Act quickly and expediently *after* reviewing the facts.

6 B. _____   Think and ponder a lot before taking action.

7 A. _____   Talk rather than listen.

7 B. _____   Listen rather than talk.

8 A. _____   Easily share my time and space.

8 B. _____   Require lots of time and personal space alone.

9 A. _____   Develop my ideas through discussion with others.

9 B. _____   Develop my ideas through contemplation.

10 A._____   Enjoy meeting and talking to people in general.

10 B._____   Keep my interactions confined to a few close friends.

11 A._____   Go where the action is. I am not bothered by activity and noise.

11 B. _____   Need my own space. To be effective, I need quiet surroundings.

12 A. _____   Speak my mind. I tend to speak before I think.

12 B. _____   Think things over. I tend to think before I speak.

13 A. _____   Enjoy surprises, like adapting to last minute changes.

13 B. _____   Dislike surprises, prefer to know what's going on.

14 A. _____   Want excitement and freedom in close relationships.

14 B. _____   Want security and stability in close relationships.

15 A. _____   Be energized by people and activities.

15 B. _____   Need to be away from people and activities to renew my energy.

Total A's _____ (Code X)
Total B's _____ (Code N)

Section 2
When receiving or processing information I tend to:

1 A. _____   Keep truth and reality as my objective.
1 B. _____   Keep harmony and understanding as my objective.

2 A. _____   Rely on logic and data to clarify my thinking.
2 B. _____   Rely on gut feelings to gain insight.

3 A. _____   Deal with people in a firm, direct way.
3 B. _____   Deal with people gently and empathetically.

4 A. _____   Be brief and concise in my communications.
4 B. _____   Be warm and friendly in my communications.

5 A. _____   Look only at the pros and cons when consid-
             ering alternatives.
5 B. _____   Consider people's needs before the looking at
             the pros and cons.

6 A. _____   Prefer to work on tasks and impersonal infor-
             mation.
6 B. _____   Prefer to focus on people and their perceived
             needs.

7 A. _____   Form and maintain relationships for logical,
             sensible reasons.
7 B. _____   Form and maintain relationships for
             emotional reasons.

8 A. _____   Be task oriented.
8 B. _____   Be relationship oriented.

9 A. _____   Maintain harmony, but can work effectively
             without it.
9 B. _____   Need harmony to remain effective in my
             work.

10 A. _____ Remain calm and cool when everyone else is
             upset.
10 B. _____ Feel other people's pain and hurt along with
             them.

11 A. _____   Have specific notions as to what's
               right/wrong.
11 B. _____   Avoid assuming right or wrong and just let
               things flow.

12 A. _____   Postpone leisure activities until my work is
               done.
12 B. _____   Look for ways to combine work and play.

13 A. _____   Respect and prefer traditional values and
               relationships.
13 B. _____   Feel restricted/confined by traditional values
               and relationships.

14 A. _____   Decide quickly and move on.
14 B. _____   Delay decisions to seek options.

15 A. _____   Look at how objects relate to and affect one
               another.
15 B. _____   Look at how objects relate to and affect me.

        Total A's _____ (Code T)
        Total B's _____ (Code F)

Section 3
When gathering and utilizing information I tend to:

1 A. _____   Use first-hand experience and direct observa-
              tion.
1 B. _____   Use flashes of intuition.

2 A. _____   Learn by specific application.
2 B. _____   Learn through general concepts.

3 A. _____   Focus on actual experience and tend to
              discount theories.
3 B. _____   Focus on possibilities and ways to improve
              things.

4 A. _____   Use my senses to know what is.
4 B. _____   Use inspiration to see possibilities.

5 A. _____   Prefer tradition and familiarity.
5 B. _____   Prefer the new and unusual.

6 A. _____   Know the practical and realistic applications
              for facts and data.
6 B. _____   Find and explore the opportunities suggested
              by facts and data.

7 A. _____   Like suggestions that are direct, practical and
              immediately applicable.
7 B. _____   Like suggestions that are unusual, novel and
              challenging.

8 A. _____   Prefer to receive and generally give specific
              information.
8 B. _____   Prefer to receive and generally give brief
              overviews.

9 A. _____   Like relationships that are constant and
              predictable.
9 B. _____   Like adventure and change in relationships.

10 A. _____   Maintain clear expectations and roles in rela-
              tionships.
10 B. _____   Keep roles and expectations flexible and
              negotiable.

11 A. _____   Work methodically, using past experiences
              and learning to guide me.
11 B. _____   Improvise to find new and better ways to do
              things.

12 A. _____   Stick to proven facts. I depend on things that
              can be clearly defined.
12 B. _____   Trust my hunches even if they don't always
              agree with the facts.

13 A. _____   Prefer work that is practical and predictable.
13 B. _____   Prefer work that is innovative and dynamic.

14 A. _____   Try to always do the right thing. I can't
              tolerate mistakes.
14 B. _____   Enjoy the experience. I consider mistakes a
              part of the process.

15 A. _____   Like schedules, timetables and specific
              deadlines.
15 B. _____   Feel constrained by timetables, schedules and
              specific deadlines.

        Total A's _____ (Code S)
        Total B's _____ (Code I)

To Tally Your Results

Total all your A's and B's in each section and transfer all your totals to the spaces provided below. Be sure to place the totals on the proper lines.

Section 1 -   Total A's _____ (Code X)
                 Total B's _____ (Code N)

Section 2 -   Total A's _____ (Code T)
                 Total B's _____ (Code F)

Section 3 -   Total A's _____ (Code S)
                 Total B's _____ (Code I)

Now, using the *code letters* to the right of each line (above), transfer your totals to the spaces below. *Circle the code letter* with the highest total in each set.

The Attitudes
1.   Code X   –   Extrovert   _____
        Code N   –   Introvert   _____

The Functions
2   Code T   –   Thinking   _____
        Code F   –   Feeling   _____

3.   Code S   –   Sensor   _____
        Code I   –   Intuitive   _____

Evaluating Your Results

Look first at the Introvert/Extrovert totals. Whether you apply an Extroverted perspective to your dominant function or an Introverted one is what ultimately determines your overall view of the world. Next, look at the four functions (Thinking, Feeling, Sensation and Intuition). Using the codes (T, F, S, I) place the *code letter* with the *highest value* in the first position below, and its opposite function in the last position. Place the code letter with the second highest value in the second position, and its opposite function in the third position.

If for example, you had totals of 10 and 5 in the Thinking/Feeling category and totals of 8 and 7 in the Sensation/Intuition category, your order would be T (total of 10) first, then S (total of 8), then N (total of 7) and F last (total of 5). See the instructions below, if you have a tie.

1. _____   2. _____   3. _____   4. _____

If you have two totals that are equal (for example; 10 in Feeling and 10 in Sensation), go back to the C.O.R.E. Temperaments profile and add values in the following manner. *(Do this step only if your totals are tied. Otherwise skip it.)*

To Break a Tie in the Functions Sections

If you had a tie in the functions sections, follow the instructions below, then re-total your results and continue.

If you are a dominant Commander (C), subtract one from the Feeling function and add it to the Thinking function.

If you are a dominant Organizer (O), subtract one from the Intuition function and add it to the Sensation function.

If you are a dominant Relater (R), subtract one from the Thinking function and add it to the Feeling function.

If you are a dominant Entertainer (E), subtract one from the Sensation function and add it to the Intuition function.

Interpreting the Function Positions

The Dominant Function

Position number one is your Dominant (or primary) function. This is the one you rely on most. When we label an individual based on the way he or she usually behaves, we are looking at a dominant function. The dominant function is concerned with the way people approach the things that interest them and with which aspects of those things they consider important.

The Auxiliary Function

Position number two is your Auxiliary (or secondary) function. This function alters your dominant one in the same way that your secondary temperament, flavors and colors your dominant temperament. This function is slightly less consciously used than the dominant function.

The Tertiary (Back-up) Function

Position number three is your back-up function. You use this function only when necessary. Normally it lies within the unconscious regions, and is activated only when you are under high stress or tension. Under extreme conditions, your conscious processes shut down to enable the "fight or flight" survival response to activate. The unconscious kicks in and your back-up function is activated.

For example, when introverted thinkers who are normally passive and reserved, get pushed too far, they will suddenly explode. In so doing, they have moved from their consciously preferred position of introverted thinker to their unconscious position of extroverted feeler, and toward an uncommon (for them) aggressiveness. As soon as they regain composure, they return to their normally passive, reserved mode again.

These occasional explosions often baffle and confuse introverted types, but the truth is, what they are doing is completely normal. Explosions can be controlled by under-standing what triggers them, and by avoiding those people and circumstances that lead to high tension, but some form of aggressiveness will always be available, because the extroverted functions, though usually unconscious and out of sight, are a part of the package.

Another example, on the other side of the coin, is the extroverted feeler, who generally loves being around people and in the mainstream. When stressed, this person will retreat from the world for awhile and seek solitude to think things out. They may get unusually quiet and sulk for awhile. Here, the unconscious introverted thinking process has taken over temporarily. But, as soon as the crisis has passed, the extroverted feeler jumps back into the main-stream again and continues on in his normally colorful, energetic, extroverted mode.

The Dormant Function

Position number four of your temperament mix is your Dormant (or least used) function. You almost never use this function, unless you call it up on purpose, to achieve a specific outcome. As soon as you have achieved it, you return this function to its dormant state.

Say, for example, your preferences mix is ITfs. (I will explain the upper and lower case letter combination shortly) This would make you an extroverted-intuitive-thinker at a conscious level, and an introverted-feeling-sensor at the unconscious level.

Sensation would be your dormant function and it is introverted. An introverted-sensor records inner responses to things, rather than recording the actual characteristics of those things. In other words, they are more aware of how the scent of a flower affects them, than of the flower itself. An extroverted-intuitive-thinker would be totally unaware of this function, and would never use it except by design.

An extroverted-intuitive-thinker normally looks at the object itself and decides what the object's purpose is (thinking) and, possibly, what it could become (intuitive projection). This type is an innovative thinker who uses external facts for his innovations, and would never use the introverted-sensation function unless he was in his normally innovative mode, trying to project how a newly invented idea, project or product might affect those for whom it is intended.

For instance, he may project how the scent of a new perfume might affect the person smelling it. A positive effect would mean sales, so calling up sensation to project a response is of value. As soon as the determination is made though, this function is returned to its dormant state where it remains unless and until something occurs that requires it to be called up purposely again.

Why Use Upper and Lower Case?

To make it easy to see how your preferences function, the C.O.R.E. MAP expresses *Extroverted* preferences in *upper case* and *Introverted* preferences in *lower case,* thus **ITfs** would signify extroverted intuition and thinking, with introverted feeling and sensation. **itFS** would signify introverted intuition and thinking, with extroverted feeling and sensation.

Return to page 161 and note your "X" and "N" attitude codes. If "X" has the highest total you are an extrovert, and your consciously used functions are extroverted (upper case). If "N" has the highest total, you are an introvert, and your consciously used functions are introverted (lower case).

On pages 178–179 is a comparison chart for comparing your two profiles. To make the comparison easier, you may want to transfer your results from page 161 to the lines below or to your journal, using the UPPER CASE = Extrovert, lower case = Introvert formula. The letter case of the first two functions will correspond to your dominant attitude (introvert or extrovert) with the last two expressed in the opposite case.

_____ _____ _____ _____
(Dominant)   (Secondary) (Back-up)   (Dormant)

Having the code letters expressed appropriately in upper and lower case in your journal will make it easier to compare your results with those on the Comparison Chart later on.

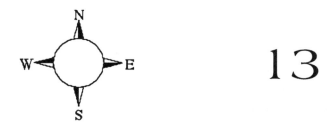

Understanding and Interpreting Attitudes and Functions

The best explanation I have seen of why the preferences are divided into two *attitudes* and four *functions,* is Carl Jung's analogy of variations in fruit. According to this analogy, a fruit can be red, yellow, orange, green and so on and it can *also* be firm or soft. A fruit of any color can be firm or soft by nature, but it can't be both at the same time. It is the particular combination of color, texture, shape, taste etc, that enables us to distinguish one fruit from another. The preferences similarly use a set of combinations to help us identify the people we encounter.

The four functions, thinking, feeling, sensation and intuition, are the processes we use to evaluate and cope with our world, and each function presents us with a slightly different view.

For example, several people may look at a beautiful yacht. One looks at this yacht and simply appreciates it for what it is. He looks at the lines, the color and the design of it. He notices how sturdy and well built it looks. He examines the hardwood deck and is impressed by the fine craftsmanship.

A second person looks at this same yacht and sees a great way to earn a living. He imagines how he might charter fishing expeditions or teach deep sea diving from the yacht. He calculates how many people he could take out on such a yacht, and how much money he could make by doing so.

A third person looks at the yacht and envisions it gliding smoothly across the ocean's surface. He imagines the wind in his hair and the smell of sea air wafting past him. He imagines the sight and sound of gulls as they swoop down to steal food from the deck. He feels the pleasure as he projects himself into the scene and lives it in his imagination.

A fourth person may look at this yacht and think how wonderful it would be to own something like this upon retirement. He may project himself forward to that time of retirement and see himself navigating the seas, visiting tropical islands, sailing friends around. Then he wonders how comfortable and economical living on a yacht might be. He wonders how dependable and seaworthy it would be in stormy weather. He wonders how much he would need to save to actually buy such a yacht upon retirement.

Each of the four was looking at the same thing, yet each one "saw" something different. Each one placed a different value on the same yacht. Their differing views are a result of different dominant functions.

The first man's dominant function is Sensation. It is the function by which we become aware of things as they appear. Sensation deals with shape, color, arrangement and facts.

The second man's dominant function is Thinking, which compares and relates things in logical sequences. It deals with how one thing causes another, and with the likely effects of certain actions.

The third man's dominant function is Feeling. This function is concerned with things in their totality, rather than with their separate parts, and with what a thing is *like,* rather than with what it *is.*

The fourth man's dominant function is Intuition, which is concerned with future consequences, and with the meaning and significance of things. It looks beyond the facts, rather than right at them, as Sensation does, and projects possible outcomes.

It is as a result of differing functions that one person will plan every minute of his day, while another just lets the day unfold naturally. One person sets out to achieve success and thinks he has a right, and maybe even a duty to exploit other people in order to reach his goals, while another sees other people as equal to himself and would never take advantage of people or treat them with disrespect. It is through differing functions that one person sees a world laden with problems and difficulties, while another sees challenge, excitement and opportunity.

Graph 1A, below, illustrates how the temperaments correlate with the early infant traits, discussed in Chapter Five. Graph 1B illustrates how the temperaments correlate with preference sets when they are unaltered by external forces.

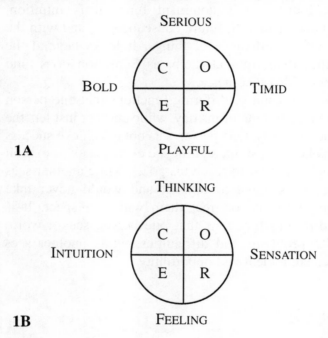

SERIOUS

C | O
E | R

BOLD   TIMID

1A   PLAYFUL

THINKING

C | O
E | R

INTUITION   SENSATION

1B   FEELING

Graphs 1A and 1B demonstrate that a bold, serious baby, unaltered by nurturing, will grow up to be a Commander, who is naturally an intuitive-thinker.

A bold, playful baby, unaltered by nurturing, will grow up to be an Entertainer, who is naturally an intuitive-feeler.

A timid, serious baby, unaltered by nurturing, will grow up to be an Organizer, who is naturally a sensing-thinker.

A timid, playful baby, unaltered by nurturing, will grow up to be a Relater, who is naturally a sensing-feeler.

A Closer Look at Introversion and Extroversion

We've looked at the four functions; now let's look at the two attitudes, introversion and extroversion, which are concerned with the way people use their energy and how they relate to the things that interest them.

Imagine two people looking at an intricately carved antique table. The first person admires the table for its craftsmanship, its design, its deep, rich color. This person appreciates all the work the craftsman has obviously put into the exquisite piece, and for her, the table is admirable in and of itself. The more she looks at it, the more she appreciates the workmanship and quality. She focuses completely on the table, and has no thought of self in relation to it. This person is an Extrovert.

The second person, looking at the same table also admires it, but she admires it for how it makes her feel and for what it can do for her. She envisions it sitting in her home in a particular place and imagines all the compliments she might get from friends and family who see it. She sees it as the perfect accent for a particular place in her home. The more she looks at the table, the more aware she becomes of her inward response to it and of the pleasure owning it would bring. While she is fully aware of the table, she is focused on her inward response to it. This person is an Introvert.

Introverts and extroverts also differ in the way they use their energy. An example of this is in the way they relate to people. Extroverts love being around people. It is through their interactions with other people and with external activities that they renew their energy, whereas introverts need time alone, without external distractions to renew their energies. People and external activities actually drain an introvert's energy.

Use the following descriptions to evaluate the preferences part of your profile. Be aware that you may not relate to the two unconscious functions (backup and dormant) because you are not consciously aware that they are a part of you. Often these are the attributes that we project onto others, rather than acknowledging them in ourselves. And because we revert to these functions only in times of high stress, when they surface, we may not like what we see. The unconscious functions are usually undeveloped, immature and archaic.

The Introverted Functions

Introverted Thinking

Introverted Thinking is concerned with *ideas*. External objects and their relationships to one another have far less importance and appeal to an introverted thinker than do ideas and concepts. Introverted thinkers use external objects and their relationships to one another only to help them formulate ideas and concepts. When introverted thinkers take note of external applications it's for the purpose of establishing an idea or concept of how things work, rather than to understand the application itself.

Introverted thinkers tend to push the limits beyond what the actual facts justify.

Mathematics is a natural area of study for introverted thinkers because numbers can be infinitely arranged and rearranged in the search for new information, and one does not need to be concerned with the numbers themselves, only with the result of having manipulated the numbers in a particular way.

Introverted Feeling

Introverted feeling is concerned with inner impressions and values, with things that are felt but are not easily expressed. Unfortunately, languages are made up of thinking terms, rather than feeling terms, and it can be difficult for feeling types to express themselves. That is doubly true of introverted feeling types because, added to the fact that feelings are difficult to convey is the fact that the inner world is an unseen (by others) world. Because expressing themselves is often difficult, introverted feeling types often retreat into a world of their own. These people often have great contributions to make to the world when they manage to communicate their thoughts, feelings and perceptions, allowing others to see way beyond the obvious.

Introverted Sensation

Introverted sensors take the details they notice and internalize them. They use external information to create internal perceptions. For example, if sunlight were shining through a prism, causing little rainbows to dance all over the walls and ceiling, an extroverted sensor would take note of the prism and would admire the depth of the colors in the little rainbows and the interesting way in which they danced about. The introverted sensor might see the dancing rainbows and be reminded of a time when he or she was at a circus as a child watching a rainbow of clowns dancing and performing in the big top. This association would bring back the *feelings* of delight associated with that earlier event and those feelings are what the introverted sensor would be aware of.

Introverted Intuition

Introverted intuition goes beyond the facts and moves to causes. If we look again at the prism-induced rainbow scene described above, the introverted intuitive would go beyond the feelings associated with the image and would look for some *meaning* to the feeling. This individual may also recall the colorful clowns and the fascination connected to that memory, but the introverted intuitive wouldn't stop there. He or she would look at why people are fascinated by clowns and rainbows and other colorful things, and try to discern the reason behind such a fascination.

An introverted intuitive probes into the very depths of the psyche, looking into the pleasures, pains, needs, drives and ambitions that motivate people and ponders the reasons for such things.

The Extroverted Functions

Extroverted Thinking

Ideas, to extroverted thinking types, have value only insofar as they relate to external objects and circumstances. They have no value in and of themselves as they do to the introverted thinking types. Where the introverted thinker is concerned with the idea itself, the extroverted thinker is concerned with the *usefulness* of the idea. That is, with how it can be applied to the external world. Ideas, to the extroverted thinker, are simply means of relating, describing and categorizing things.

The extroverted thinker also looks at and uses the ideas of other people only when he or she thinks those ideas have merit, and merit is determined by whether or not the extroverted thinker takes the other person seriously or respects that person's position. Introverted thinkers look at the idea itself and think it should be considered no matter where it came from.

Extroverted Feeling

The extroverted feeling function is the means by which we value other people and other things that exist outside ourselves. That value is seen as external to self and is not connected with internal responses.

It is by the extroverted feeling function that one can say, "I don't like that person, but I respect his work and the good it has done," or "I have no use for that object, but I can see how it could be valuable to someone else." Extroverted feeling types move into relationships with other people easily. They decide whether to build or continue a relationship based on their general feeling about the other person, rather than on the facts.

Extroverted Sensation

Extroverted sensation is the function by which we observe things as they actually are. This is the function that enables us to become aware of the physical arrangement of things around us, of the facts as they present themselves, and of the circumstances and events around us. Obviously, this is an essential function, but when used in the extreme, users of this function become so wrapped up in the facts or the unfolding of events that they are unable to separate themselves from them and so become subject to them. Their moods are dictated by whether or not things are going well outside themselves, and by whether or not the condition of the world is "good" or "bad." They can't imagine how someone could be happy or content when the world is in distress or when the people around them are not behaving in an acceptable manner. As you might imagine, an individual whose sensation function is extroverted is prone to wide mood swings since the external world is constantly changing.

Extroverted Intuition

Intuition, like sensation, is also concerned with the way things are. But, where sensation looks at the external events themselves, extroverted intuition views external events and then uses them to discern what *caused* the event. In other words, it takes the external event and looks beneath it, rather than directly at it. Where extroverted sensation looks at the behaviors of people and at how their behaviors lead to a particular outcome, extroverted intuition looks at the motives behind the behaviors of people and projects outcomes before they are actually realized.

The Western world is dominated by the left brain functions of sensation and thinking. The thinking/sensation combination allows those who function from external data to make judgments about people's motives and about what causes certain events to evolve in the way they do. On the surface this seems like a more consistent and reliable way to gather and process information, but there is plenty of evidence that indicates that this method is no more reliable overall than are the internally-focused, right-brain functions of feeling and intuition. We can be just as mistaken in drawing conclusions from what we detect in the outer world as we can in using our intuition and feelings to look beyond what seems obvious to assume outcomes. One function is really not more accurate or reliable than another, each simply uses different means to reach an end.

A clear example of this is the differences between the highly scientific types, who function from the external thinking/sensation realms, and the highly religious or spiritually oriented types, who function from the internal feeling/intuition realms. Since they each see the world and process what they see differently, it is highly unlikely that these two groups will ever completely agree.

Knowing the attitudes and functions will give you a better understanding of yourself, of your world view and interpretations and of how the people in your life may differ from you. Recognizing that people are different, but not necessarily wrong, enables us to cope with our differences better and can improve our ability to relate to others effectively.

It is now time to look at the comparison chart to see whether your temperaments profile and your preferences profile match. The chart on the following page lists the preferences combination first, the meaning of that combination second, and the corresponding temperaments combination third.

(Note: The letters in parenthesis and marked with an asterisk * at the end of each set are provided to allow you to cross-reference the preferences, as presented in the C.O.R.E. MAP, with the corresponding letters assigned by Myers-Briggs. If you have taken the Myers-Briggs Type Indicator (MBTI) and have your test results, you can use this second set of letters to compare your C.O.R.E. MAP preferences to the Myers-Briggs Type Indicator. This second set will also be helpful in learning more about yourself through the study of books that utilize MBTI designations.)

C.O.R.E. MAP Comparison Chart

Commander Combinations

TIsf – Extroverted TI, Introverted sf =
      True Commander (ENTJ)*

TSif – Extroverted TS, Introverted if =
      Commander/Organizer (ESTJ)*

STfi – Extroverted ST, Introverted fi =
      Commander/Relater (ESTP)*

ITfs – Extroverted IT, Introverted fs =
      Commander/Entertainer (ENTP)*

Organizer Combinations

tsIF – Introverted ts, Extroverted IF =
      True Organizer (ISTP)*

tiSF – Introverted ti, Extroverted SF =
      Organizer/Commander (INTP)*

stFI – Introverted st, Extroverted FI =
      Organizer/Relater (ISTJ)*

itFS – Introverted it, Extroverted FS =
      Organizer/Entertainer (INTJ)*

Relater Combinations

fsIT – Introverted fs, Extroverted IT =
      True Relater (ISFP)*

ifTS – Introverted if, Extroverted TS =
      Relater/Commander (INFJ)*

sfTI – Introverted sf, Extroverted TI =
        Relater/Organizer (ISFJ)*

fiST – Introverted fi, Extroverted ST =
        Relater/Entertainer (INFP)*

Entertainer Combinations

FIst – Extroverted FI, Introverted st =
        True Entertainer (ENFJ)*

IFts – Extroverted IF, Introverted ts =
        Entertainer/Commander (ENFP)*

SFti – Extroverted SF, Introverted ti =
        Entertainer/Organizer (ESFP)*

FSit – Extroverted FS, Introverted it =
        Entertainer/Relater (ESFJ)*

Do Your Profiles Match?

The temperaments profile will match with the preferences profile if you are interacting, orienting your
world, presenting yourself and processing information in
harmony with your nature. When the two match, you
know you are working with, rather than against, your
natural inclinations.

Sometimes the results of your preferences profile will
indicate a true type from within a temperaments combination type (an Organizer/Relater combination on the
temperaments profile and True Organizer on the preferences profile, for example). This simply means you are
using that temperament fairly heavily, and this should *not*
be considered a mismatch.

If the two do correlate with one another and you are having difficulty in certain areas of your life, the difficulties are most likely due to the broader-based value systems you grew up with, as opposed to individual beliefs about yourself. Value systems are broader and more general than personal beliefs. They affect the way you view the actions and behaviors of others and of societies as a whole, as much as they affect your beliefs about yourself. These, like personal beliefs, are stored as subconscious programs that affect our overall reactions to the world we live in, rather than affecting our basic nature. We will look at these more closely soon.

If Your Two Profiles Don't Match

Look at some of the possible causes for discrepancies on the following pages to try to determine *why* the results of your temperaments profile didn't match the proper preferences set. Knowing where the discrepancies are will give you some very valuable insights as to where you need to be focusing your attention, in order to get headed down the right path more quickly.

Where there is a mismatch, *both* of the profiles should be examined. The temperaments profile can be off when you don't know yourself due to a difficult childhood that moved you away from your nature and altered your perception of self. In this case, your answers reflect your false beliefs, rather than your reality. If you feel a general discomfort about your life, which seems to revolve around yourself rather than around other people's behaviors, this is probably the case.

The preferences profile can be altered when you have been dealing with difficult and restrictive circumstances for an extended period of time. We almost always shut down our conscious thinking processes, and revert to the unconscious functions when we are in distress. This can be for just a few minutes, such as when we are confronted with danger and move to the fight-flight-freeze survival mode, or it can last longer. Jung referred to the state of being completely unaware as "unconscious," and it is possible to remain in this "unconscious" mode for years, because of high stress situations that continue for that long. When this occurs, you can remember when you were different. You may or may not like the "self" you used to be, but you do remember being a different kind of person at an earlier time, and you can probably pinpoint the reason why you are now functioning differently.

A man, fifty-five years old, who attended a self-discovery workshop recently, gave very definite visual (non-verbal) clues to the fact that he was a Commander by nature. His preferences profile showed him to be a Commander, because he was still relating to the world according to his nature. But his temperaments profile showed him to be a Relater, which is the complete opposite of the Commander. I questioned this, telling him that his non-verbal communications were those of a Commander, and asked him why he identified with the Relater. He answered that he used to be like the Commander, but eighteen months earlier he had changed. As a Commander, he had functioned on the negative side, and he didn't like what he had become. He described his "old self" as a selfish, materialistic drunk. He said he had turned his life around when he "hit bottom," and was now trying to develop his spiritual side. He saw the Relater behavior as "spiritual," because it was the extreme opposite of what he had been before. When I asked him if he was *comfortable* in Relater mode. He said, "Not especially, but I think I need to be this way to develop my spiritual side and get away from my past behaviors."

I suggested he begin to look at, and develop, the positive aspects of the Commander while he was working to eliminate the negative ones. He said he would try, and the following week, when the class met for part two of the workshop, he reported that he had been studying the positive aspects of Commander all week. He said that when he projected himself into positive Commander mode, rather than Relater mode, he felt happier and more energized. He could now see how he could move away from his destructive behaviors without having to "put a damper" on himself.

In another case, Sandy, a woman in her late thirties, had similar results, but for very different reasons. The results of her temperaments profile was Relater/Organizer, while her preferences profile results were Commander/Entertainer (the extreme opposite of the temperaments outcome). Like the man in the earlier example, her non-verbal communications revealed her to be a Commander/Entertainer, and I asked her why she was identifying with the Relater/Organizer profile. She too reported that she used to be like the Commander/Entertainer and had *loved* it. But two years earlier her financial world began to fall apart. She lost her business and a lot of assets, and was still struggling to get back on her feet. During this financial loss she had also lost a significant love relationship, and now felt like she was in a tailspin.

Sandy longed to be her "old self," but feared she never again would be. I assured her that not only would she be, but that she was really still her old self. She had switched to the unnatural mode as a defensive measure, and had remained in that mode for two years! Just knowing that her old, beloved self was still hers to claim turned her life around. She realized the strengths and attributes she had drawn on in the past were still hers to draw upon and she began to move back into her true mode. Her energy level shifted upward visibly, and she reported that it felt like a thousand pounds had been lifted from her.

A mismatch of the two profiles can occur for a number of reasons, many of which are listed on pages 187–191.

Let's use Sandy's example to help you decipher your own differences, if your profiles don't match one another. In Sandy's case, her temperaments profile was off. Her correct profile should have been Commander/Entertainer (C/E). The preferences set that matches the C/E temperament is ITfs. This is what her preferences profile resulted in. She was still functioning and expressing in her naturally preferred mode of extroverted-intuitive-thinking. But, the preferences profile that matches her assumed temperament of Relater/Organizer mode is sfTI, which is a mirror image of her correct match. Here, introverted-sensational-feeling would be necessary to have a match, and she was clearly an extrovert.

Usually a complete reversal, such as this, has apparent causes, but to find the cause may require examination of several areas. In the explanations of possible causes, which begin on page 187, an individual with such a reversal would first determine which of the two possible profiles seems most accurate by reading the overview sections of both profiles. Then, working from the assumption that the one that feels most accurate overall is the correct one, the individual would examine the sections that corresponded to the seemingly correct (matching) profile.

Again, using Sandy's example: Her temperaments profile result was Relater/Organizer, which matches the sfTI preferences set. However, Sandy's preferences profile result was ITfs, which corresponds to Commander/Entertainer. Her journal worksheet would look like this:

	Temperament	Matching Preferences
Profile 1	Relater/Organizer	sfTI
Profile 2	Commander/Entertainer	ITfs

As you can see, the preferences sets are mirror images of one another. Relater/Organizer is an introvert and Commander/Entertainer is an extrovert. Relater/Organizer is high in sensation (s) by nature, while Commander/Entertainer is high in intuition (I). Relater/Organizer functions predominantly in feeling (f) mode, while Commander/Entertainer functions predominantly in thinking (T) mode.

Sandy now needs to decide which of the two profiles seems most accurate *overall* by reading the overviews for each set. If profile one (Relater/Organizer – sfTI) was determined to be the correct one, she would check for possible causes under the headings of *If your matching profile is "N" but you were high in "X"; If your matching profile is "S" but you were high in "I";* and *If your matching profile is "F" but you were high in "T."* If profile two (Commander/Entertainer – ITfs) was determined to be correct, she would check *If your matching profile is "X" but you were high in "N"; If your matching profile is "I" but you were high in "S";* and *If your matching profile is "T" but you were high in "F."*

To look at a less extreme example, assume that your preferences profile resulted in TSif (which is the matching set for Commander/Organizer) and your temperaments profile result was Commander/Entertainer (which matches the ITfs preferences set). In this instance, the thinking function is conscious and extroverted, just as it should be, in both profiles. The variation is between the intuition and sensation functions. Here you would look at the totals for both Entertainer and Organizer (Commander in the dominant position matches in both profiles) and check to see how close they are. If they are very close (less than three apart), you may be switching back and forth between both temperaments, because you feel you need to develop behaviors that are not natural for you. It may be the social aspects that are natural to the Entertainer, for example, or it may be the organizational abilities that are natural to the Organizer. Begin by determining which of these two aspects you have to work hardest to maintain. The most difficult to maintain is most likely the part that belongs in back-up mode, rather than in a primary or secondary position.

If the two totals are *not* close, something else is going on and you will need to refer to the *possible causes* pages as described in Sandy's example above.

To begin your comparison, in your journal place the preferences code that matches the result of your temperaments profile, next to the temperaments result, as was done in Sandy's example. In the above example the Commander/Entertainer result in part one would have ITfs (its matching preferences set) written beside it. Next write out the matching temperaments set beside your preferences profile result. In the above example TSif would have Commander/Organizer written beside it.

Now, go back and read the overviews for both temperaments to determine which of the two seems to describe you most accurately. In the above example you would read both Commander/Entertainer and Commander/Organizer.

Assume the profile which most closely describes you is the correct one and work from there in looking for a possible cause for the incongruity between the two profiles. If, for example, you determined the Commander/ Entertainer set best described you, then the ITfs preferences set would be the matching code and you would want to check *If your matching preference is "I" but you were high in "S"* to find possible causes for the incongruent profiles.

If the preferences portion of your profile is incorrect, you are functioning contrary to your nature in the way you relate to and interact with the outside world, but you are aware of your true nature. You may be consciously choosing to function in an unnatural mode for a specific reason.

If the temperaments portion of your profile is incorrect, you are relating to the world according to your natural inclinations. You may not, however, be consciously aware of your true nature and, if you are aware of it, you are not relating to it for some reason.

By discovering the possible causes of the variation, you can begin to bring your nature and your nurture into alignment purposefully. Doing so will bring faster results and will enable you to be more accepting of current conditions, knowing they are temporary and fixable.

If the two temperaments are completely incongruent, or if *neither* profile seems to fit, you may want to enlist the help of family and friends who know you very well, in reworking the two profiles. You may also want to re-take the temperaments profile from the position of what type person you would be if you were living your ideal life, and to re-examine the questions in the temperaments profile. This may not give you an accurate result, but it will get you headed in the right direction. If, after these steps have been taken, you are still uncertain, write me at the address listed in the back of this book and I'll send you a questionnaire to further define yourself, and information on how to get a personalized assessment of your results.

I know this seems complicated, but keep at it. The result you will achieve is worth the work. Close self-examination and the comparison of the two profiles have helped many of my students discover their true natures and move purposefully toward them. I have seen students go from shy, backward and insecure to bold, assertive and confident in a very short time as a result of applying this self-discovery process.

It isn't uncommon to see an introvert, who has been miserable trying to live up to the expectations of an outgoing parent or a society that honors extroversion, learn to enjoy being quiet and introspective.

I have had clients, who had been in counseling for years trying to get their "problem" fixed, breathe great sighs of relief in realizing that their only problem was trying to be something they were not.

One such client had been trying to live up to his powerful father's expectations all his life and genuinely thought he was flawed in some way. When he discovered that his approach to life was perfectly normal for an introvert, he was able to like and accept himself. He also recognized that his father's unrealistic expectations of him were really his father's problem, not his own. In understanding this, he was eventually able to let go of the expectations, and progress in a way suited to his introverted nature.

Possible Causes for Profile Variations

Examine the possible causes for variations listed below to see if you can determine why your two profiles were different. Chances are you will understand why the differences exist almost immediately, even if the specific cause isn't listed. Just knowing some of the possible causes for variations is usually enough to pinpoint what is happening in your own life.

If your matching profile is "X," but you were high in "N"

It is possible that you were nurtured into a passive or submissive role as a child and haven't yet overcome the effects of the contrary nurturing. If this is true, you probably have an intense longing to be more extroverted and sociable than your internal programs are allowing at this time.

Another possibility is that in the recent past, you pushed yourself too hard and are now experiencing "burnout." In this case, you have purposely chosen to withdraw at this time and, although you know the time will come when you will again want to enter the mainstream, for now you are content to be more reclusive than is the norm for you.

If your matching profile is "N" but you were high in "X"

It is possible that you were nurtured into a more aggressive role than is natural for your basic temperament. This can sometimes happen when parents are over-achievers and expect the same from their children. If this is true for you, you probably feel very pressured to perform and may even feel manipulated by one or both of your parents.

You probably push yourself to the point of discomfort on a fairly regular basis and long for a time when you can just retire from the "rat race" and take life easy. Your idea of a perfect retirement is likely to be a quiet little cottage in the country, away from the hustle and bustle of the crowds, or a travel trailer that allows you to move around the countryside at your leisure.

Another possibility is that you have bought into the American societal ideal and believe that you have to be an extrovert in order to fit in like you want to. In that case, you probably coach yourself on a regular basis in order to keep yourself interacting with others in an open and extroverted way. Extroverted behavior is something you taught yourself and, even though it seems to require regular effort on your part, you feel it serves you well and so you continue to make the effort.

If your matching profile is "T," but you were high in "F"

This may indicate that there is something going on in your life that's causing you to move temporarily away from your naturally preferred thinking mode and into the normally less preferred feeling mode.

Is there anything currently happening in your life that might cause you not to trust your thinking faculty right now? Perhaps you made a real blunder recently using the thinking faculty, or perhaps you have just found (or lost) the love of your life and your feeling side is more prevalent than usual. Perhaps you are basking in the joy of having just become a new parent. Perhaps you are dealing with the pain of going through a divorce, grieving the loss of a loved one, mourning a failed business or dipping into the feeling side of your nature for some other specific reason.

If your matching profile is "F," but you were high in "T"

If you find yourself in thinking mode when your correct profile indicates you should be a "feeler," it could be that you have moved to thinking mode temporarily in order to protect yourself, or possibly because you think that you need to be in thinking mode right now. Sometimes the breakup of a marriage or other significant relationship will cause an individual to move to thinking mode in order to deal with it in a stoic manner. Men often take this approach more than women. Women tend to feel freer to grieve over a loss, thereby staying in feeling mode for a while, whereas men tend to try to divert themselves and to "be strong."

A new job or job position that requires a great deal of thinking can move a feeling type to thinking mode until they get more comfortable with the position. Even a decision to get one's life and affairs in order can move an individual to thinking mode while the planning and organizing is going on, since these activities are predominantly thought-related.

If your matching profile is "I," but you were high in "S"

Intuitive people tend to *internalize* information, where sensors look at the *external* world. If you are using your external senses when your nature is to rely on your intuition, it may be that you grew up in a family that valued external processing and tended to discount or ridicule "hunches" and intuition. If this is so, you will discover some amazing things if you decide to let go of the early programming and develop your intuitive side!

Another possibility is that you are currently in a position where it is important to you that you pay closer attention to your external world rather than relying on the "less concrete" intuitive processes. This sometimes occurs when someone is learning a new job or job position (such as having moved into management recently) and is not yet secure enough with his knowledge or skills in this area to rely on intuition, or when the job requires a lot of attention to details and any assumptions could lead to disaster.

If your matching profile is "S," but you were high in "I"

This is less commonly seen than the reverse, but it does occur occasionally. In this instance an individual who would naturally use external information becomes more introspective and tends to use hunches and intuition instead. This sometimes occurs when individuals retire and feel they now have the luxury of getting to know themselves. It is also seen occasionally in individuals who have experienced some kind of crisis in their lives, which has caused them to step back and re-evaluate. Typically, this re-evaluating is done on an internal level, and even a person who would normally be an external sensor will temporarily move to the internally oriented intuitive mode. Sometimes people switch to the intuitive mode when working on developing their spiritual side and feel they need to learn to trust their inner selves more.

Summary of Nature and Nurture

1.   Temperaments refer to natural, in-born traits. They are at the very core of your being. Your happiness and contentment in life are directly related to how well you are functioning in accordance with your temperament.
2.   Preferences refer to the way you use your energy and relate to others (introvert and extrovert), the way you process information and make judgments (thinking and feeling), and the way you view the world and become aware of situations (sensation and intuition).

3.   Ideally, and under normal circumstances, the prefer-
      ences function in accordance with the temperaments
      and are a natural extension of them. However, pref-
      erences can be altered by circumstances and by will.
      If they have been altered during childhood by
      negative influences, they are likely to be acting as a
      mask to cover natural attributes that didn't seem
      safe to use as a child. If they were altered in
      adulthood, it is usually an attempt to deal with a
      stressful situation or to reverse our direction in life.
      Developing and moving toward the positive traits
      that are natural to your temperament may be a more
      effective way of achieving the outcome you are
      after.

4.   To find our ideal path and walk it, we must first be
      self-aware. Through awareness of self, we are able
      to move purposefully toward our nature, integrating
      those aspects of nurture that serve us well and elim-
      inating or diminishing those that do not. As we do
      so, our nature begins to emerge more fully, our
      temperaments and preferences tend to align them-
      selves and we cease to feel lost and confused.

Action Plan

1.   Be sure you know and understand your basic nature
      (temperaments) as well as your preferences before
      you continue on. If you are unsure about your
      results, ask someone who knows you well to help
      you with the profiles. Then combine your own gut
      feelings with the information they give you.

2.   Create a general outline of yourself in your journal.
      List the likes, dislikes, strengths and weaknesses

that are inherent to your personality, then decide which strengths you want to begin building upon, and which weaknesses you will work to diminish or eliminate. Just knowing what your particular attributes are can get you headed in the right direction, but consciously working to improve them will put you miles ahead of where you have been, and turn you more surely in the direction of your ideal lifepath.

Recommended Reading:

- *Type Talk,* by Otto Kroger and Janet Theusen
- *Do What You Are,* by Paul Tieger and Barbara Barron-Tieger

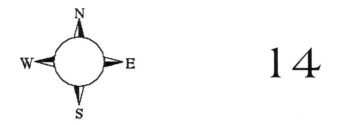

Values and Beliefs — Your Guiding Principles

In *First Things First,* author Stephen Covey states that we are really not in control of our lives, our principles are. He suggests that this idea "provides key insights into the frustration people have had with the traditional 'time management' approach to life." I would add that it provides key insights into the frustrations people have had with their lives as a whole!

Our principles, in the form of values and beliefs, are extremely powerful determinants of behavior. They are the magnet which, when functioning correctly, keeps the compass pointing true North, and when malfunctioning, keeps us going in never ending circles, lost, confused and confounded.

Our values, beliefs and guiding principles are what gives us a sense of direction and a sense of self. They tell us who we are within the larger context, what we are capable of, and what our purpose in life or mission is. They decide whether what we do or observe is good or bad, right or wrong. They tell us how we should behave from moment to moment, and how we should live our lives in the long term. They tell us how we should treat other people and how others should treat us.

In fact, our value systems are so powerful that they can either completely overshadow and even sabotage our conscious thoughts and desires, or they can lead us to heroic heights. James Allen, author of the classic book *As a Man Thinketh* writes, "The within is ceaselessly becoming the without. From the state of a man's heart proceeds the conditions of his life; his thoughts blossom into deeds, and his deeds bear the fruitage of character and destiny."

The states of your heart and mind are directly related to the state of your values and beliefs. It is through the consistent and almost automatic application of our values and belief systems that we create our lives for good or ill. Personal attributes determine the *content* of your life; values and belief systems determine the *quality* of it.

Examples of values and belief systems overpowering or sabotaging conscious desires are everywhere. A man loves his wife and children and consciously wants to take care of them, love and nurture them, but his belief system tells him his only worth is in what he earns, so he works long hours, including weekends. He comes home so exhausted that all he wants is to be left alone. He snaps at his wife and children when they attempt to get some of his time or attention, then feels guilty for it. That isn't the way he wants to treat them, but what can he do? He's tired and their need for attention is just adding to his level of exhaustion. He never gets quite rested before it's time to go back to work and start all over again. His wife and children feel neglected and unloved and the relationship begins to deteriorate. The very thing he thinks he is working so hard for is slowly, but surely, slipping away.

But you see, he only *thinks* he is working hard for his family. He is really working hard to comply with a value; his unconscious belief in what is necessary to prove his worth as a man.

A woman consciously wants to be honest and forthright. She admires people who openly express their wants and needs, and she tells herself that's the kind of person she wants to be. But her unconscious beliefs tell her she has value as a woman only if she behaves in a docile "feminine" way. Her fundamental upbringing has taught her that a "good" woman surrenders her own wants and needs for the good of others, so she ignores her desire to stand up for herself and speak her mind. She marries a man who orders her around and ignores her needs. She is miserable and longs to be free to live her own life, but another of her values tells her she cannot divorce this man, no matter how unhappy he makes her.

Because she bought into these beliefs long ago, she doesn't even think to question them anymore. That's the way it is. God ... the church ... Mom ... society ... somebody decreed this was right. She doesn't even remember now who sold her the idea, or when. She doesn't know that her life is being controlled by a set of beliefs that are not serving her best interests. She doesn't know she has the ability and the right to change them, if she chooses. She is consciously aware of only one thing ... she is not happy.

Where do these erroneous beliefs, which keep us miserable and off track, come from, anyway? Why do we let them control us? Why do we allow the "shoulds" and "ought-tos" of other people to dictate our behaviors and rule our lives to our own detriment?

Values and principles fall into the nurture category. Quite early in life we begin to gather information from our parents and other family members, teachers, friends, churches, societies, and any other people or systems with which we interact on a regular basis, in an effort to discover who we are and what life is about. We are most influenced by the people and organizations we believe we can trust.

Research over the years has pointed to the fact that most of our values and beliefs are formed by the time we reach the age of ten. For many, that means some ten-year-old is running their life for them, and they don't even know it. Many of our values and beliefs develop before we even have the ability to reason, so it isn't surprising that many of them don't serve our adult needs very well.

A parent tells us we are incompetent or lazy; a teacher tells us we are poor at math or English, or that we talk too much; an older sibling teases that we are clumsy, lanky, ugly, inept. Everyone keeps defining us in derogatory ways and we believe them. We buy into the false information, because we are too young to know that what we sometimes do isn't really who we are, and that the across-the-board assessments of us are not the truth.

How we apply the values and beliefs we buy into, and which ones we choose to keep and use, may be determined to some extent by our nature, but once established, they move to automatic mode and literally run the show. For that reason, it is vitally important that your journey toward personal awareness, happiness and contentment include a thorough examination and evaluation of your values and belief systems.

We seldom question the validity or rightness of our values and beliefs unless something emotionally significant occurs to cause such questioning (like a death in the family, divorce, turning forty, an illness, or perhaps even hearing an inspiring story or reading something that starts us thinking and searching).

I suggest that you really look at the beliefs you hold sacred, and try to uncover the ones you may have never even thought about before. Take them out and examine them as an intelligent adult, rather than as the child you were when you bought into them. The examination process can uncover some very deeply held beliefs. You will most likely become aware of values and beliefs you will want to keep and enhance, and you may find some that are definitely not beneficial.

For most of us, the idea of having the equivalent of a child running our show isn't a very comforting thought, but to eliminate something that isn't working we must first examine the nature of the problem at its root. Those old, outdated programs can cause all kinds of misery in our adult lives, and if not examined and updated, the childish programs keep running rampant.

If there are aspects of your life (your thinking processes, feelings, behaviors, attitudes, principles or lack of them, etc.) that are causing you problems on a fairly consistent basis, and you find you are functioning true to your nature, it's very possible those difficulties are a result of functioning through childhood values and beliefs that have become automatic programs.

For example, say that your mother taught you to always clean your plate and you bought into that belief system as a child because "happy plates" always brought smiles of approval and praise. But now, as an adult you are seventy-five pounds overweight and really want to reduce. You eat out a lot and no matter how much food is served, you find yourself gorging to clean your plate. You leave the restaurant feeling both physically and mentally uncomfortable because once again you have over-eaten. You didn't mean to and you just don't understand why you keep doing it. All you know is that you just can't leave food on your plate. Consciously, you beat yourself up and tell yourself you must stop doing that, but as uncomfortable as you are with the excess weight and the repeated failures, you never stop.

That is a childhood program that is no longer serving you well. However, until you recognize it as such and take specific steps to change the programming, you will continue to over-eat, gain weight and beat yourself up for having "no willpower." The truth is, willpower has nothing to do with it!

You see, humans are primarily emotional beings and the sub-conscious mind runs predominantly on emotions. When we buy into something, we buy into it at an emotional level and the "purchase" is stored in the subconscious for future use. Since the emotional, subconscious programs are far more powerful than the logical, conscious thinking processes, you have no hope of winning that battle until you rewrite the subconscious program.

There is hardly any area of your life that is not affected to some extent by your early programs. The trick is to find out which beliefs are now detrimental to you and to discover what is at the core of each of these errant belief systems. *Forget* willpower and concentrate instead on finding and rewriting the internal programs that no longer serve your needs.

The programs that cause us consistent problems and emotional pain are usually easy to recognize. In fact, we often know exactly what these programs are, we just don't know how to eliminate them. It isn't uncommon to have workshop participants tell me that they continue to be attracted to the wrong love partners, because they remind them of a parent who they felt never loved them. Or someone might say that they are afraid of conflict, because they had an aggressive parent who frightened them, or punished them when they tried to defend themselves. Others report that they can't leave a bad job or marriage because a parent taught them it was wrong and weak to abandon their commitments.

Fear of people, such as was the case for me, is a very commonly reported problematical program. This particular fear can show up in many forms, from social shyness, to defensiveness, to bullying people to keep them from getting too close. I have a client who wants desperately to find someone to love and be loved by. She is thirty-six years old and has never been married. In fact, she has never even had a romantic partner. Not one. She is a very attractive woman who should have no trouble attracting a romantic partner, but she has a program that won't allow it. At the age of nine this lovely young lady was molested by a family friend. He told her it was her own fault, because she was so pretty that he couldn't help himself.

Now, twenty-seven years later, she dresses very plainly and broadcasts nonverbal messages that scream, "stay away!" to everyone. Whenever she is approached by an admiring male, she retreats, either physically or emotionally. As badly as she wants love at a conscious level, she continues to send out "stay away from me" messages, so no one dares approach her.

Her programs say, "Men mean pain. If you let yourself be pretty, you will get hurt and it will be your own fault. You don't deserve to be loved. You are 'used goods.'" These are her own words. She knows what the messages are. She knows the source of the problem. She has known for a long time. She just never knew she could rewrite the program. She has spent years trying to eliminate these programmed messages with logic, to reason her way out of them. The problem is that they were not created by reason and they will not be cured by reason either. They were created emotionally, stored as emotion, and they are activated by emotion-producing stimuli. No amount of reason will (or can) cure them.

Creating New Programs

The first step in the reprogramming process is to identify the beliefs that make up your values. So before you go any further, take the time to list in your journal all the beliefs you can call up. Core beliefs are usually very broad in nature. Sometimes they seem reasonable, and sometimes they seem to have no real value and cannot be validated by actual facts.

For example, "People should be treated with respect," is a generally beneficial belief, although it can be taken to extremes. People who are abusing you do not deserve respect. Other healthy beliefs, kept in proper context, might be: "I should behave appropriately in public places. I should eat right and exercise to guard my health. I should try to resolve problems without resorting to aggressive behaviors. I should honor my parents and other superiors. People shouldn't be kept waiting. People should maintain a certain degree of cleanliness."

It's easy to see how any of these, carried to extremes, could cause problems, however. "People should be respected" could translate to, "Never upset anyone or assert a different opinion; it's disrespectful." "I should behave appropriately in public places" could translate to extremely reserved behaviors that won't allow you to be playful or even comfortable around other people. "I should honor my parents" might result in avoiding a parent that you don't, in fact, honor. In such a case, avoidance is less painful than admitting lack of honor, because that would violate the belief. "People shouldn't be kept waiting" might create extreme impatience and little tolerance on your part when someone else is late. Or it might make you a slave to the clock to the point of absurdity. "People should maintain a certain degree of cleanliness" could translate into a compulsion on your part, causing you to be overly neat and clean; you run around after everyone, wiping tables, washing dishes as fast as they are dirtied, washing your hands, etc.

There are value-based beliefs that would seldom cause problems, unless taken to great extremes. Many of these are spelled out in religious literature, perhaps because they are so timeless and limitless. Beliefs such as, "I should not steal. I should not kill my fellow man. I should respect and care for the planet I live on. I should respect myself. I should be truthful." Beliefs such as these only become problematic when we change the "I" message to a "You" message and start to judge other people, imposing our own beliefs on them.

Other belief systems are decidedly harmful. Some of these are beliefs such as, "I am worthy only if I am loved by others. I am not as good as other people (or as pretty, smart, talented, handsome, athletic, etc.). I should never disagree with my parents. If I haven't made it by the time I'm forty, I'm a failure."

Do you recognize any of these? If so, write them down. Some other areas you may want to consider in listing your broad-based beliefs are, "What do I really believe about the way I should eat? When, how and how much is it all right to sleep? How and when should I work? How should money be spent or saved? How and when should I play? How should I relate to family, friends, superiors, co-workers, subordinates, friendly strangers, unfriendly strangers? How should I present myself to the world? What should a man be like? What should a woman be like, or a wife, a husband, a daughter, a son, a parent, a child, a boss, an employee, etc.? What about your religious faith, your family, your town, city, state, country, the government. What "shoulds" have you attached to these? Where did you get those notions? Are you happy with them? Do they serve you well? Do they make you happy and content? If not, why are you keeping them?

Action Step: Updating Values and Beliefs

1. List your basic values and beliefs in your journal, then write out the answers to the following questions. Examine each one closely and answer it as completely as you can.
2. Who tends to determine what the agenda will be in any given situation? Do you usually decide or do you leave it up to someone else? Why?
3. How does this relate to how you behaved at home or to how you observed your parents acting? Are you modeling a parent? Rejecting a parent's example? Sometimes we begin modeling a parent early in life. Then, as an adult, our role and that of the parent are very similar, even if we don't like the way that parent behaved, or the way we are behaving now. Or

we may reject everything that parent stood for, perhaps even some good things that might be beneficial to us.

4. How do you tend to resolve conflict? Do you attack or do you withdraw? Are you still using the same techniques you used as a child or has it changed? If it has changed, how? Are you acting true to your nature? (Commanders and Entertainers usually move toward aggressive, and Organizers and Relaters usually withdraw or become passive/aggressive. Assertiveness is a better option in both cases.)

5. What role did you play in your family as a child? Are you still playing it today? Some commonly played family roles are: advisor, baby, bully, captain, cheerleader, entertainer, director, dutiful helper, happy-go-lucky clown, leader, loner, nobody, organizer, parent substitute, peacemaker, producer, provider, show-off, the smart one, the star, tag-along, tattletale, team player, weakling. You will discover, as you think about your role as a child, that it closely parallels the role you feel most comfortable with now and is the role you often resort to when under stress.

6. What values and beliefs did you adopt from your family? How many views and beliefs do you share with your parents? Why do you think this is so? What was the highest unspoken value in your family when you were growing up? Was it to be (or appear to be) rich, to be (or appear to be) happy like Beaver Cleaver's family ... the perfect picture? Was it to embrace the world or was it to trust no one? How did your family's values and beliefs affect the way you show affection, relate to authority figures, view

and approach food, relate to money, view the roles of men and women, view success? How have they affected your work ethic?

7.   Work through the values and core beliefs. How did you get them? Who taught them to you? Whose voice do you hear as you recall these messages? Mom's? Dad's? Grandpa's? Who? Try to remember events and interactions from your childhood that might have created the values and beliefs you now hold.

Action Step: Uncovering Old Programs

Some values and beliefs may be hard to uncover because we seldom, if ever, question core beliefs. It may be helpful to begin by looking at the areas of your life where you are experiencing discomfort or responding negatively on a fairly regular basis (anger, frustration, guilt, fear, loneliness, etc.).

From this starting position you can try to recall childhood events that will uncover the source of the current belief, habit or pattern. Be sure the memories are your own and not based on stories you have heard from family members. The ones that are yours will have an emotional aspect to them. These are the most important to recall, because you own these, and it is that ownership that is causing you to continue using these memories.

For example, when you feel frustrated, why are you feeling that way? What triggers frustration in you? What triggered it in you when you were small? Can you remember a time when you felt frustrated under similar circumstances as a child? What happened? Record the memory. Try to recall as many incidences as you can, recording a minimum of three.

Any memories you can recall that occurred before the age of six will be especially helpful. These early memories relate in some way to a core belief that is actually a survival message you created, and upon which you are more than likely still acting. It is very rare to find someone who is not still acting on their primary survival message when we do this exercise in workshops.

Even memories that seem irrelevant have a survival message in them. One woman in a self-discovery workshop recalled only happy events that centered around her birthdays. She was doted upon as a child, and her birthdays were always special events. She had big parties and lots of presents. She remembered her parents and grandparents being at her parties making her feel very special. She couldn't see how there could be any survival message in such pleasant memories. Upon closer examination, however, she saw that the survival message was, "Love equals very special birthdays." In realizing that this was a survival message, she understood why she had broken up with every man she had ever dated. None of them had cele-brated her birthday in a "very special" way. Therefore, they couldn't possibly love her. Love meant life to her and she had been very miserable without it. No telling how many men she had tossed out because they didn't love her in the "right" way. That is, they didn't throw lavish birthday parties for her.

As soon as she understood how flawed the belief was, she stopped assuming men didn't care for her if they didn't honor her birthday properly. The last time I talked to her she was in a very good relationship and had made it past a birthday that she and her new romance had celebrated, by going to dinner and a movie — no big parties, no lavish gifts, no making over her in any unusual way. And though she was aware of a slight (and decidedly childish) disappointment, she knew the source and, this time, it didn't trip her up.

1. In your journal, write out any memories you can recall right now, then state what the attached emotion is. You will find the memories tend to have a theme of sorts. That is, they seem to have something in common; a common feeling or message, like the birthday parties, in the earlier example.

2. Try to determine what the core belief behind the memory is. For example, middle children sometimes have a core belief that says, "I am nobody. Just a number." People who had very domineering parents who didn't tolerate children well, might have a core belief that says, "Survival means being very flexible, never making any waves, remaining as invisible as possible."

    If you have a good memory for the events of your childhood, you may be able to easily recall events that led you to certain conclusions and beliefs. But, if you are like most people, a little jogging of the memory may be helpful. If that happens to be the case, the exercises listed in the recommended books may help. In general, go back to your preschool years and try to relate memories to specific events, like birthdays, Christmas, Easter, moving from one house to another, going to preschool and so on. These events may help you with recall. Or use the questions below to help jog your memory.

    • What was your usual mood as a child? (Happy, sad, frustrated, anxious, fearful, confident, etc.) Why?

    • Do you remember your parents spending much time with you? Was the time pleasant or problematic?

- How did you picture your parents as a child? (Dependable, angry, absent, weak, strong, manipulative, helpful, etc.) What was your overall impression?
- Did you argue with either of your parents? When? Why? What was the result?
- What frightened you as a child?
- What were some embarrassing moments you can recall?
- What made you feel proud or happy?
- Were either of your parents domineering or overly permissive?
- When challenged by a parent, did you give in or fight back?
- How were you treated when you were sick?
- How were you treated when you achieved something?
- Did you have playmates? What did you play?

3. Record any additional childhood memories the above questions may have elicited. You might find it helpful to use the following format.

Memory # 1: _____

_____

The most significant part of this memory is:

_____

The strongest emotion attached to this memory is:

_____

The assumption at the core of this memory seems to be: _____

Use as many sheets of paper as needed. Continue with memory two, three, four and so on (as many as you can recall) using the same format.

4. After you have reviewed the memories, answer the following questions:

A. What do the behaviors you recognize from the childhood memories have in common with your adult behaviors? Were you an angry child and are now an angry adult? Were you hurried as a child and now impatient as an adult? Did a parent terrorize you as a child and now, as an adult, you can't cope with authority figures?

B. As you recall these memories, how do you feel now? What emotions do these memories evoke? (Anger, frustration, happiness, comfort, fear, pride, embarrassment, etc.) What do all the memories have in common with each other? How might the view you had of your family be affecting your family interactions today? Your relationship with your spouse or your children?

C. How might these memories answer the following questions about yourself? What kind of person am I? What does being this person mean? What must I do to thrive in this world? What must I do to survive? What behaviors are acceptable? What is unacceptable? What is good to do? What keeps me out of trouble? What is bad to do? What gets me into trouble?

5. What negative self-talk can you identify? (These will be messages like "I am really dumb," or "I should accept only the very best," or "People should know how I feel," or "People shouldn't upset me," or "I'm so fat and ugly."

What could you change such statements to that would be more positive and would get a better result? For example: "I am really dumb" could be changed to, "I don't know everything, but I am far from dumb" "I should accept only the very best." could be changed to, "I deserve good things as much as anyone else, but I can't know what 'best' is so I'll work toward getting good outcomes." "I'm so fat and ugly" could be changed to, "It would be nice to be thinner and prettier in a society that values such things, but I know that beauty is more than skin deep, and I have some very good attributes. People who know me and care about me, love me for what I am, not how I look. Character lasts a lifetime, while looks always diminish, so I'll focus on, develop and value my character."

If you can't hear what it is you are saying to yourself, try determining what you are focusing on — what emotions (fear, frustration, anger, disgust, impatience), what expectations (shoulds and ought-tos), what assumptions? (I never get anything good. People are dangerous. Most people are idiots! My family expects too much from me, etc.)

Do you focus on worst-case scenarios, always imagining the worst possible outcomes? Do you focus on dire consequences, creating do-or-die choices and horrible repercussions that are sure to befall you if you choose wrong?

You may notice some resistance to the childhood memories exercises. Stay with it, though; it shouldn't take more than an hour or two, and it's a very effective way to "clean" your mental house. You may want to repeat portions of the exercise in the future to see whether you can recall more, but one thorough examination can be amazingly effective in unclogging old beliefs. Once you get the process going, the mind seems to realize that many of the old, long forgotten programs are no longer useful, and they often just pop into your consciousness to allow you to examine them.

As you begin to recall old beliefs, you may become aware of a critical voice or a frightened child, or a shamed child, or an angry teenager. We all have many aspects of ourselves and these can take on a seeming life of their own. Beliefs often function within subconscious loops that form patterns or programs. And because the subconscious mind thinks in symbols (such as people, animals, familiar objects, colors, etc.), these patterns or programs often take on personalities, much like the characters in your dreams do. This is especially true of the programs created from beliefs we adopted as children, and have never really questioned or checked for validity as adults. We adopted most of these to protect or direct ourselves in some way. The subconscious mind takes the belief, creates a pattern in which the belief can function and assigns it a label, an identity, so we can call it up by name, just as you call up a file in a computer by name. Only the subconscious "names" things by way of an identity or image, as opposed to a title or name. These files then appear as "other selves."

The roles of these "selves" remain unchanged as long as they are unquestioned or unchallenged. It doesn't matter that you are an adult now and the patterns were formed when you were a child. As far as the subconscious mind is concerned, these patterns or programs were created to protect and direct the child and, since there has been no new data added to the original, they are still protecting and directing the child. Only now the child has an adult body and an adult mind from which it could function if the programs didn't get in the way.

Unfortunately, the programs don't tend to sit quietly and let us go about our adult business without their interference, unless and until we begin to rework them on purpose — to add new data. We change the data and add new information by gaining an awareness of the programs that now exist and then introducing new, adult-level facts to them.

Some of the societal values we buy into should suffice as examples. Society presents us with many messages in direct or indirect ways. Those we buy into and fail to question can, and often do, become sources of discomfort and difficulty for us. At a societal level we buy into messages such as, "You have to be attractive to be acceptable." This belief makes billions of dollars for the grooming, cosmetic and weight-loss industries and billions more for counselors. It does very little, however, for the individual who believes the way they look is the measure of their worth.

Another societal belief we often buy into is, "Money and power equals success." The result of buying into this belief too heavily is high stress, emotional strain, fatigue, self-castigation and overwork.

Some of society's values conflict, causing us to be pushed one way, then pulled another. Women can't be too powerful and men can't be too emotional. We are supposed to be independent, but we ought to conform. We have to be educated, but we aren't supposed to think too much. We ought to be friendly and helpful, but we should avoid strangers. To be of value we must achieve, achieve, achieve, but be humble. We should build our lives around the opinions of others, but be sure to be your own person. The mixed messages are endless. No wonder many of us feel so lost and confused.

Most of my clients come to me for counseling, coaching or training because they have bought into societal or family values that they can't possibly live up to. They feel inadequate, insecure and unsure of themselves until they begin to discover what is real and important to *them,* and what is not. To make those discoveries and gain the subsequent freedom, we generally need to do some "house cleaning."

Clearing out the old to make room for the new is as important to forward progress as is discovering your true self. The true self can't emerge past a pile of garbage. And that is exactly what all the old, detrimental beliefs and values are: just so much garbage, but it is powerful garbage. It has taken on a life of its own and it thinks it is you. Worse than that, you may look at the garbage and think it is you, as well. It isn't. There is nothing about the real you that you won't like.

To rewrite the programs that often show up as sub-personalities, we must learn to either work with or around them, or to transform them. If we don't, they can become great deterrents in our efforts to grow and to move forward in our lives. Transformation is often the better option when the program presents itself in a negative or limiting way, such as a frightened child, a critic or a big, black wall that feels like fear.

Whatever form the program takes, we transform it by updating its data to match the present reality. In effect, we help the child within to grow up. Then our beliefs and behaviors cease to exist as "childish" and begin to present themselves in more emotionally mature ways.

Note: If you found it difficult to complete the action steps in this chapter, because you can't seem to hear the things you tell yourself on a regular basis or you can't recall your childhood, I would highly recommend that you buy and work your way through the book, *Embracing Our Selves,* by Hal Stone and Sidra Winkleman. This book will help you identify your various "selves" and learn how to hear and evaluate their dialogue. Once you are aware of what is going on inside your mind, you can go to work to alter the beliefs and values to better suit your current needs.

To help you recall your childhood, you may want to get and work your way through *Unlocking the Secrets of Your Childhood Memories,* by Dr. Kevin Lehman and Randy Carlson.

Action Step: Hearing and Acknowledging Your Whole Self

1. If you are already aware of the dialogue that you carry on with yourself, begin listing in your journal all the "selves" you can identify. You may be aware of a critic who tells you all the things you do wrong and informs you of all the things that you "should" be doing better. You may be aware of a nurturer who tells you how capable you are, and who gives you strokes when you do something right. You may be aware of a frightened or insecure child who dares not take a risk. You may recognize a shamed child, filled with guilt and remorse over some past misdeed, either real or perceived. You may become aware of a free child who is happy, playful and spontaneous, or would like to be. You will likely be aware of the adult self, who is logic and reason personified. You may discover other sub-personalities, as well.

   Everyone has five basic "selves," according to Eric Berne, the developer of Transactional Analysis. Berne's work is based on therapeutic interpretations of the various ego states or "selves" which are responsible for particular behaviors and responses in people.

These ego states or "selves" can be observed to be directly responsible for the way people act in their "transactions." In any given transaction, which Berne described as the basic unit of social interaction, each individual behaves and reacts to others as either a child (the emotional self), a parent (our beliefs, "shoulds," "should-nots," and "ought-tos"), or an adult (our logical, rational, mature awareness and cognition).

Both the child self and the parent self have two aspects, or sub-selves. The child presents itself as the Free Child (the unaltered self, which you were born to be) and the Adapted Child (the child self after adapting to socialization, training, parental messages, and the various criticisms we are subjected to throughout life). The parent presents as the Critical Parent (which tries to protect by pointing out negatives and limitations) and the Nurturing Parent (which encourages by pointing out positives and potentials).

According to Berne, we are born with the Free Child self and quickly adopt the parent selves from our own parents or other significant relationships. The parenting (whether negative or positive) causes the adapted child to develop. Adaptation can be either good or bad. Good adaptation is what enables you to function effectively within a society. It prevents you from stealing or killing, from running around naked or doing other inappropriate things in public. Bad adaptation can take the form of fear, guilt, painful programs, social shyness, communications difficulties and a hundred other troublesome or painful things.

By uncovering these "selves," you can discover their purposes and find ways to better utilize them by asking them direct questions. To begin this process, create a dialogue section in your journal and write both the question you ask the self and the response you get. You will be amazed at how much insight you can gain through this type of journaling.

Remember that when you are addressing emotions, such as fear, anxiety, shame, or guilt, you will be addressing the Adapted Child self. When you address criticism of any sort, you are addressing the Critical Parent self. These two feed off of one another, so where the presence of one is high, the presence of the other also will be high. The Critical Parent harshly chastises the Adapted Child, which is already frightened or guilty or ashamed, and the chastisement makes the Child feel more insecure, causing the dominant feeling to intensify. As the Child begins to feel even more frightened, guilty or ashamed, the Critical Parent sees an even greater need to shape it up and so criticizes all the more. This vicious cycle continues until you, the adult, intervene. You intervene by focusing on the more positive aspects of self and looking for facts about yourself and your abilities that will invalidate the Critical Parent's assumptions. Identify and learn to listen to the voice of the nurturing parent. The positive messages and cheering on you will get from this aspect of yourself can diminish the role of the Critical Parent and bring it into its proper role of protector.

In addressing your joy, your playfulness or any of the positive emotions you would like to develop, you are addressing the Free Child self. In addressing your potentials and positive qualities, you will be addressing the Nurturing Parent self. Your Adult self is unemotional. It is pure logic and observation.

2. Take the time to identify your selves and to get to know each of them. Use the positive ones to help you develop and reinforce the positive traits you would like to have. The nurturer can diminish the effects of the critic, for example, if you begin to focus on the nurturer's messages, as opposed to those of the critic. Most of us are really good at hearing the critic. Learn to hear and pay attention to the nurturer until the critic assumes its proper role.

The "negative selves," their resultant emotions and self-talk have little apparent value to you, but you will not want to eliminate them. You simply want to change them. They have a valuable role when they are in their proper places. The critic is actually a protector gone awry. When it is assigned its proper role, it is very helpful in warning us of danger and helping us to avoid potentially harmful situations.

The frightened child is the emotional self that wants to love and be loved. When properly nurtured, it becomes a healthy emotional state that can love others without conditions or strings attached, and can give you complete faith in self and self-acceptance.

As you dialogue your way through the various sub-personalities, you'll discover that your self-talk is a sort of self-coaching device that enables your subconscious to hold onto and reinforce whatever belief systems you hold, whether they are beneficial to you or not. To the subconscious, they are all beneficial or they wouldn't be there. It's up to you to sort them out.

The process of changing unwanted belief systems begins with identifying them and then changing the self-talk or focus connected to them. Just the act of becoming aware of the "selves" and accepting that they have some useful purpose can be helpful. But taking the time to find their purpose and help them do their jobs better often yields fabulous results. By working with the various sub-personalities, which are the keepers of your basic belief systems, you can transform your negative beliefs to more positive ones. Positive belief systems will serve you well. They can speed your journey to your ideal path, and keep your course direct and true.

Action Step: Re-Evaluating and Updating the Programs

1. Write out any conclusions you have come to as a result of your childhood memories exploration and exercises.
2. State what you believe to be the true purpose of each of the "selves" you have become aware of. (Remember: The purpose is always a *positive* one even if the programs appear as negative right now.)
3. Create a journal section for each "self" you have identified and continue your dialogues. Be sure to write out your questions and the answers you

receive. This will help you gain insight as the
dialogue continues over time.

4.   Lay out the old programs you created as a child and
      look at them with the eyes of an adult. Realize you
      have the ability to re-create them. As an adult, you
      have the right and the privilege of parenting yourself
      now. Give yourself permission to do that and begin
      to nurture the "selves" that feel frightened, insecure,
      ashamed or unworthy, in the way you would like to
      have been nurtured all along.

5.   Transform the critic by directing and encouraging it
      toward its rightful role of protector.

6.   Develop the nurturing self and allow your whole
      being to benefit from the nurturer's positive
      awareness of your capabilities and potentials.

Remember, every aspect of yourself (all the "selves"
you have created) are attempting to work for your benefit.
They acknowledge and work toward the fulfillment of two
basic subconscious needs: your survival and your
happiness. When you have a clear picture of what constitutes survival and happiness to you (the authentic you),
every part of your being will go to work to help you achieve
it. That's their role. It's what they do! Give them the right
tools, show them the right path, and watch them go! When
you clearly see and acknowledge (both consciously and
subconsciously) what your ideal lifestyle should be, every
part of your being goes to work to achieve the new goal.
Then it's just a matter of time until the ideal is also the
reality.

Recommended Reading:

- *Unlocking the Secrets of Your Childhood Memories,* by Dr. Kevin Lehman and Randy Carlson
- *Emotional Intelligence,* by Daniel Goleman, Ph.D.
- *Why You Do What You Do,* by Bob Biehl
- *Embracing Our Selves,* by Hal Stone, Ph.D. & Sidra Winkleman, Ph.D.
- *Embracing Your Inner Critic,* by Hal Stone Ph.D. and Sidra Stone, Ph.D.
- *Self Parenting,* by John K. Pollard, III

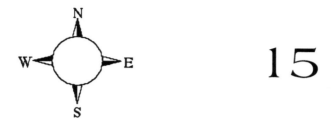

Building the Bridges

> *"Pollution is nothing but the resources we are not harvesting. We allow them to disperse because we have been ignorant of their value."*
>
> Buckminster Fuller

Sometimes we preview the traits we think we have available to us and see mostly garbage, so we assume we have nothing to build upon. This may have been your position in the past, but in the process of working through this book you should now have a whole list of good things to begin building with. You may have uncovered a lot of things you really don't want anymore as well. Some of these things you will certainly want to toss out, but some of what now seems undesirable can actually be quite useful, when properly applied. So, our next step is to sort out and recycle the good stuff and use it to build some important bridges.

You will want to eliminate all the old belief systems that have held you back over the years and kept you lost.

And you will want to toss away some of your resultant responses (shame, guilt, fear, etc.) But you can recycle a lot of the attributes that are there for your benefit, but which have been misused or misapplied in the past. Fear is an example of something that you might, on the surface, want to eliminate. But fear is your fight-flight-or-freeze survival response. It keeps you alive and out of harm's way when properly applied. It only keeps you imprisoned and limited when it's misapplied.

Many of us misuse or misapply a lot of potentially good things, and we also carry around an awful lot of stuff that we don't really want and can't use anymore.

We hold onto things like guilt, shame, resentment, anger, intolerance, old grudges, shoulds, ought-tos, musts, cannots and on-and-on. I suspect that if we had to carry around the physical equivalent of all this mental and emotional garbage, most of us wouldn't be able to lift it. Even at the mental and emotional levels it can feel rather heavy. Maybe it's the weight of all this excess baggage that keeps some people feeling tired, listless and drained so much of the time. Other people also see and feel the effects of it. They are visible to the eye, the ear, the heart, the soul, the psyche, and just about every other part of our being. Every slight, every insult, every dishonest act, every guilt trip, every injustice — in fact, every negative thought or action that we experience and then impose on others is the direct and visible result of all the garbage to which we insist on clinging.

Besides the negative actions and responses we direct toward one another, we also toss our garbage around in other visible ways. Our posture, facial expressions, tone of voice and gestures all speak volumes about the mental and emotional debris we carry around. It can droop shoulders as well as attitudes and expectations. It causes pain — mental, emotional and physical — and creates depression. It drives us to the point of exhaustion, causes us to blow up too easily, and creates a thousand and one other problems, for ourselves and others.

On the other hand, people who have managed to discard all the old, negative, useless stuff present themselves as mentally and emotional healthy adults. They are generally kind, helpful and considerate of other people, and delightful to be around.

Negative beliefs always produce mental and emotional garbage, which leads to low self-esteem, which results in poor relationships, which result in friction and trouble.

No one really wants to hang on to negative beliefs. Those who do simply don't know how to change or eliminate them. However, there are some very specific steps we can take to move away from negative outcomes, and you've taken some of them already by recognizing outmoded beliefs and patterns, and identifying traits and attributes you want to develop. In completing each exercise, you are taking action that is purposeful, and your persistence will eventually lead you to your ultimate goal.

We need persistence, real determination and a willingness to move into areas of *discomfort* to eventually find that place of great comfort and joy. If you allow for times of discomfort and, possibly, temporary setbacks or distress, they won't trip you up when they appear. And they will appear. Expect them. Welcome them. Then move through them and come out on the other side a better, stronger person.

The next step is to gather your tools and resources together, set your sights on your probable path, and set out on your adventure. Along the way, we will be building bridges and clearing away the debris that now blocks your way. Once on the path, you'll have all the tools you need, including your indispensable compass.

But, before you can get to your ideal path, we'll need to build some bridges across the gaps that exist between where you are now and where you really want to be. And, to do that, you'll need some tools and some additional information.

Armed with an awareness of your true nature, you will need to position yourself firmly, in order to develop a high level of confidence. To do that, you will need some strong *personal boundaries.* So, get out your journal and let's build bridge number one.

Action Step:
Building Personal Boundaries

1. Go back to the original entry in your journal, which should be *all the things you would try, if you knew you couldn't fail.* Do you want to add anything to this list? Do you want to eliminate any of it?

    When the list seems complete, list the attributes it would take to actually achieve these things. If, for example, you had on your list, "Climb Mount Everest," you would want to list attributes like a sense of adventure, courage, fortitude, persistence, good planning, willingness to take risks, etc.

2. Once you have listed the attributes necessary to complete each of the activities you named, make a list of those that appeared more than once. You may have identified courage as necessary to six of the activities, for example, so courage would go on the list.

3. Now draw a great big circle in the middle of a blank page in your journal. Inside the circle, write "I AM." Outside the circle, write "I AM NOT."

4. Inside the circle, list every *positive* attribute you currently recognize in yourself. List all the things that make you feel comfortable, content and happy. List all the things you like in the list of attributes that are natural to your temperament. Then list all the attributes you identified in step two.

5. List all the negative things you see in yourself, and all the things that make you feel uncomfortable, constrained and unhappy *outside* the circle.

What you now have inside the circle will serve as your new personal boundaries. You can add to or remove entries in the future, as your awareness grows, but what is here now will be your starting point.

I know, you are protesting that the attributes from your "If I knew I couldn't fail" list aren't really yours. But, they really do belong to you or you wouldn't have the desire to own them. You may not have them *developed* yet, but they *are* yours to develop. Remember, this is your starting place. You will build on this foundation, which will become the basis of your courage and confidence as you move toward your ideal self.

We must know who we are and who we are not, in order to move through life with confidence. How can we take a stand, state a firm position or hold our own with confidence, unless we know what our position is? This is possible only when we have strong personal boundaries. Without them, there are no guidelines and no road signs to follow. And, if we have nothing to point the way, we inevitably get lost.

(Your personal boundaries are the signs and markers that keep you moving in the right direction.)

We can't feel confident when we're lost. Personal convictions and principles (boundaries) give us a sense of direction and purpose and, with these, the confidence to proceed. They even help us to set realistic, achievable goals, by defining what realistic and achievable for us really is.

6.   Take a look at what's inside your circle. How does ownership of those attributes make you feel? How does owning what's outside the circle make you feel? Decide right now that the qualities *inside* the circle are exactly what the label says; they are what you are, and what's *outside* the circle is what you are not, and never again will be.

It's all right to feel a little unsure right now. Defining your boundaries is just the first step. To gain confidence in this new self-image you will need to practice functioning from this image, just as you have practiced functioning from the old, erroneous one. The next step is to take ownership of your true self — the self inside the circle — and to build the bridge of confidence based on this truer, more beneficial image.

Action Step:
Building the Confidence Bridge

The formula for confidence is:
Knowledge + Experience + Positive Feedback =
Confidence

Confidence is a result of knowing what we are supposed to be doing and how to do it well. This requires much more than just gathering knowledge. Knowledge, in and of itself, is next to useless. It only becomes useful and powerful when it is *applied*. That is the *experience* part of the formula.

There are all kinds of examples of where knowledge alone can't create confidence. In fact, all of life demonstrates this truth. Can you be a great and confident tennis player if you have only *read* about the game, but never actually played? How about a dancer, painter, typist, engineer, manager? Not likely! We only gain confidence by applying the knowledge.

Positive feedback comes as a result of continually applying knowledge to build experience, and allowing ourselves the latitude to adjust and re-adjust our experiential outcomes until we get a good result. No one is perfect on their first attempt at something. Most of us never get perfect at all, but with practice we can become good enough to receive positive feedback and develop a reasonable degree of confidence.

1. From the list inside your personal boundaries circle, choose what you consider to be the most important attribute or action for you to take. Begin gathering the knowledge you still need in this area, if any, and then begin developing and improving this attribute or action through experience. Look for ways to apply it until you feel proficient. The positive feedback will come with every improvement you yourself notice, as well as from the compliments of others. You'll soon discover that the positive feedback you give yourself is what brings the most rapid results.

2.   Look at other areas of your life where you feel confident and competent, and see how you applied knowledge and experience in those areas. How long did you persist before you received any positive feedback from self or others? Why did you persist? Use the same formula to develop confidence in each new endeavor.

3.   To assure your success in each new endeavor, learn to consciously apply the *no-fail formula*. You have used it all your life at an unconscious level, now move it into your conscious awareness and use it on purpose. The best way to remember this formula is to think " Triple A."

The Triple A, No-Fail Formula is:

Attempt to achieve something.

Assess the results of that attempt, and if you don't like the outcome,

Alter your approach.

If the new result still isn't what you want, make a new attempt and assess the new results. If you still don't like the outcome, make another alteration. Continue this procedure until you find the right formula and get the outcome you want. If you keep at this, you cannot fail!

You have no doubt heard the story of Thomas Edison and his 10,000 formulas. It is said that a reporter once asked Edison if he felt like a failure. Edison had tried, as the story goes, several thousand formulas to create a light bulb and had failed on each attempt. To the reporter's inquiry Edison replied, "No, my good man, I do not feel like a failure, for I have not failed. Quite the contrary, I have succeeded in finding several thousand ways not to make a light bulb."

Edison, was using the Attempt, Assess, Alter formula. He would try a certain combination of chemicals, and if these didn't give him the result he was after, he would examine why this combination didn't work and make whatever alterations he assumed would help. He would then try the altered ingredients. When these didn't work, he would examine how and why they didn't work and make another alteration. He reportedly repeated this process nearly 10,000 times before he succeeded!

You've been using this formula, too ... all your life. Everything you have ever accomplished was accomplished just this way. You learned to walk, talk, read, write, drive, reason, make decisions, everything that way! It has worked for you even though you may not have known what you were doing. Think how powerfully it can work for you when you apply it on purpose!

So, set grand goals, dream big dreams, and keep using that formula to come up with the means to reach them. Keep moving forward with confidence. Be willing to "fail" in order to succeed. It has been appropriately suggested that if you aren't failing at something, you aren't trying. See failure as proof that you are at least trying, and embrace it. Use failure as an indicator to let you know when you are off course. Once you begin to see "failure" as a valuable tool, and perhaps even as a friend, you'll know its appearance simply means it's time to look for ways to alter your course, and you'll keep trying until the absence of "failure" tells you you've got it right. Stick to the formula and you must succeed eventually.

A good example of using "failure" properly, is sailing. When a sailor sails into the wind, there is only one way to keep the ship moving forward ... the sailor must "tack." If you are unfamiliar with sailing, tacking into the wind is a process of zig-zagging back and forth in order to catch the wind in the sails. It is a series of left-to-right course corrections that are executed to get you to the intended spot on shore. But, there's more to reaching the right destination than just knowing how to correct the course. It's also necessary to know when and how much to correct it. That can only be determined when you know your destination. That's why it's so important to have strong personal boundaries and clearly defined goals.

Suppose the sailor in our example had an idea where he wanted to go, but thought he should be able to get there more quickly and easily than was practical. Suppose he could see his intended destination, but thought he should arrive there with only three or four corrections. If after the fourth correction, he decided to give up because his experience didn't match his expectations, he would never reach his goal. He would have failed simply because he quit making corrections too soon.

Knowing our destination or outcome in advance is just part of the formula. Once the destination is clear, we must start moving toward it, correcting and re-correcting all along the way, until we reach the goal. By deciding to make as many alterations as necessary, and never giving up until the goal has been achieved, failure becomes impossible. Your life may run out before you achieve the full result you wanted, but as long as you are moving in the right direction, you are on the path to success!

Action Step: Bridging the Abyss of Fear

Although the fear of failure can be a major deterrent to personal growth and accomplishment, it is by no means the only form of fear that will hold you back and keep you from realizing your potential. Other common forms of fear that can be just as paralyzing and limiting are fear of ridicule, fear of rejection, fear of embarrassment and fear of confrontation. There are others, but these are the biggies.

Fortunately, there are effective ways of dealing with fear. You can never totally eliminate it, nor would you want to. It is useful when our lives are in danger, but can be quite a nuisance when it goes awry and starts controlling our lives in non-life-threatening situations. For example, if you are headed to a party and on the way there, begin to get knots in your stomach and to feel nervous and anxious, then the fear you are dealing with is inappropriate and limiting. It is not serving you in any useful way.

Or say you hate your work environment and really want to find, or create, a workplace better suited to you. You don't take the necessary steps, however, because you are afraid you might fail, get fired or be disappointed in whatever new environment you might find. Again, fear has been misapplied and has become a source of limitation. Your life is not endangered by looking for better work; therefore, the fear you are feeling is invalid.

To eliminate invalid fears and move to a place of confidence, there are some specific steps you can take. This is an ongoing process, but keep at it. Overcoming limiting fears is vital to your forward progress.

1. Learn to recognize the signals your body sends you when in the grips of fear. (You will feel a knot in your stomach, your heart racing, your breath getting shallow, muscle tension, etc.) Close your eyes and imagine a fearful scenario right now. Put yourself right in the middle of it and make note of your bodily responses. Write down the specific symptoms that appear, such as shoulder tension, butterflies in your stomach, sweaty palms, trembling or throat constriction.

2.   Begin to notice when you are feeling these fear responses and then ask yourself, "Is this fear valid?" If your life, or the life of someone else, is not in danger, the fear is not a valid one.

3.   If the fear is not valid, realize that the source of the fear is in your thinking processes, rather than in the situation. Then move to the source of the problem, your thinking processes and your self-talk.

4.   Notice what you are saying to yourself. You may become aware of statements such as, "I just can't do that. What if I fail? I'd be so embarrassed I would just die!" or "I always say something stupid. I'd better not speak up." If you are unable to hear the actual words you are saying, try to determine what you are focusing on. You'll probably discover you are focusing on dire consequences or worst case scenario. Take the example of not speaking up in a group meeting. You may not be able to hear the dialogue that you are carrying on with yourself, but you may be aware of your expectation of embarrassing yourself.

5.   Begin to look for other options. It's true, the worst could occur, but so could the best, or anything in between. We create fear by looking at only one option, the worst one. Find as many other options as you can, and then choose one you can believe in that won't induce fear or disbelief. Often the best case scenario will shut you down as quickly as the worst case, because you don't believe it to be a possible outcome.

      Going back to the "can't speak up" example; the worst case is that you speak up, make a total fool of yourself, and the embarrassment is so acute your heart stops and you die! That's pretty extreme, but that's what your subconscious mind does with worst case scenarios and dire consequences; it takes the scene all the way to death, and where death is certain, fear is appropriate!

The best case scenario might be that you speak up and say something truly profound and everyone in the room is so impressed that they immediately begin to worship you. The first scene shuts you down due to the fear response. The second one is tossed out as an impossibility, leaving only one other option, the first one, which the subconscious has already determined would surely end in death. The result is, you do nothing.

There are other options. You might speak up and say something stupid or trite, be embarrassed, and not die. You may determine to use the experience to apply the Triple A formula, for a better result next time. Or you might speak up and say something just as sensible as anyone else in the room, and not be embarrassed at all. The others may or may not like your comment or suggestion, but you still spoke your mind and you feel better for having done so. Or you may speak up and make a really good suggestion that is appreciated by at least some of the group. What options can you find that are believable enough to allow you to take action now?

6. *Do* the thing you fear and, as Emerson so aptly stated, "the fear will disappear." The fastest, surest way to eliminate disabling fear is to take calculated risks in the areas directly related to your fear.

If, for example, you fear embarrassment, you purposely put yourself into potentially embarrassing situations. The fact that you plan the action and expect to survive the embarrassment will enable you to maintain better control. More often than not, you will discover that the actual experience isn't nearly as bad as the imagined one was! Every time you take such a risk, you expand your comfort zone to a new place and, as your comfort zone gets larger, the fear gets smaller until, at some point, it's gone! Try it. It works.

It is also easier to eliminate fear if you remain focused on what you are trying to achieve. Let's look again at the earlier example of going to a party. Say you decided to go to the party in spite of the fear you felt. If you don't have a plan for what you intend to accomplish at the party, it is unlikely you will manage to eliminate the fear, because every assumed outcome is one of disaster. You could change all that however, if you set a goal and had a plan, such as trying to meet at least three people at the party. Now you arrive at the party with a mission, a goal, something to do when you get there. You'll be focused on your mission rather than on the fear. If your goal is just to meet three people and you take the initiative to approach and meet three, you will have achieved your goal no matter what the outcome is. Every time you set a goal to do something new, like meeting new people, and follow through on it, you get a little better at it. As you get better, your confidence increases and, before long, it's a piece of cake!

7.   Realize that you are worth all the time and effort it might take to get past the fears and move into a position of confidence. Take the time. Make the effort.

Action Step:
Building the Relationship Bridge

As we approach our ideal path and it begins to come into clearer view, we realize that we can't and really don't want to travel our path alone. We are going to need, among our tools, those things that will help us to develop and maintain our relationships more effectively. For most of us, the most important factor in measuring our level of happiness is to be found in our relationships. Good relationships are what make life worth living and the journey we are on meaningful. Without them, who would cheer us on when we're winning and encourage us to keep going when we're losing?

Good negotiators know that when it comes to dealing with people, knowledge is truly power. The more we know about people, the stronger and more effective is our position. This truth extends beyond negotiating and into virtually every area of human interactions.

You probably recognized a lot of the people you know and learned something about them when you took the temperaments and preferences profiles. These are extremely useful for helping you to understand others more fully. You will definitely want to continue studying them and applying your knowledge to the people around you. Many people tell me these two profiles have been the most useful tools they have ever used in helping them to understand other people and deal with them effectively. Understanding temperaments and preferences is a powerful aid, but you also will benefit by an awareness of basic wants and needs. Knowing what people want and need can give you additional information to apply to the benefit of everyone.

Psychologists have identified seventeen basic wants and needs. They are basic because virtually every normal person has them. Knowing that everyone wants and needs the same basic things makes it much easier to help others get their needs met. In the process, you will get many of your own needs met, as well. The ability to help one another is the basis of every successful relationship, whether personal or business-related.

You don't need to memorize the seventeen basic wants and needs, but an awareness of them can give you an edge in relationship building. And, since a large part of your overall happiness will revolve around the quality of your relationships, this knowledge will be of great benefit.

The Seventeen Basic Wants and Needs:

1. Survival (food, clothing, shelter, air, water, etc.)
2. Safety (for self and family)
3. Comfort (physical and psychological)
4. A sense of personal power (mastery of self, others)
5. Ego gratification (a feeling of importance)
6. Financial success (money and all it will buy)
7. Recognition of efforts, reassurance of worth
8. Social or group approval, acceptance by one's peers
9. The desire to win (to be the first or best, to excel)
10. A sense of roots, of belonging
11. The opportunity for creative expression
12. The accomplishment of something worthwhile
13. New experiences, adventure
14. Liberty, freedom and/or privacy from intrusion
15. A sense of dignity and self-respect, self-esteem
16. Love in all its forms (romance, friendship, family, community)
17. Emotional security (freedom from stress or conflict)

As you might imagine, your basic nature will affect the intensity with which you want or need any of the above basics, but you will discover that each of them applies to some degree. You may realize that your need for freedom is somewhat greater than your need for roots or belonging, for example, or vice versa. But you still need both of them to some extent.

Communicating by Type

You have undoubtedly had the experience of trying to communicate something to someone who simply cannot seem to comprehend what you are trying to say. Or perhaps they are trying to tell you something that you can't comprehend. Either way, if we aren't communicating effectively we aren't really connecting with one another, and connecting is crucial to the building and maintenance of relationships.

It isn't all that uncommon to get befuddled when people are talking about a subject we are unfamiliar with. But, what about when people start talking about things we do know about and we *still* can't understand them? They are speaking English and we are speaking English, but somehow we are not speaking the same language. What's going on?

There are lots of reasons, from poor listening skills to lack of interest, but cross communications are often a result of different communication styles. Each of the four temperaments has a preferred style and they use that style almost exclusively. The temperament that is opposite our own is usually the most difficult to communicate with and, unless we learn what the differences are and compensate for them, the communications problems are likely to continue.

I am surrounded by Organizers. My husband and all three of my children have strong Organizer traits. I have next to none. They like to give and receive a lot more detail than I usually want. I have learned to be patient and listen a little longer than I'd like, and they have learned to make their explanations a little shorter than they would like. When I'm the one giving the information, I tend to overview, giving too little detail. They usually stop me, back me up and ask for clarification and details.

Good communication takes work. The work is a whole lot easier when you also have some knowledge of what other types of communicators want and expect from you, so let's take a look at how the four temperaments communicate.

Commanders don't care for the social chat. They want direct, concise communication. They want you to say what you want, get to the bottom line and let them get on with things. They are decisive and direct, they don't appreciate people dancing around an issue.

Their opposite type is the Relater. Relaters want, even need, to dance around issues. They don't like getting to the point and getting out! They think doing that is cold and harsh. But, no matter, to communicate with a Commander effectively, you'll need to get to the point as quickly and directly as possible.

Organizers want lots of information: facts, figures and details. They don't want any stone left unturned. They want specifics, and they want everything to tie together in a logical way. The more specific the information, the better. They don't like overviews or generalities.

Their opposite is the Entertainer, and Entertainers hate details. So when the Organizer starts giving long, detailed explanations, the Entertainer checks out, either mentally or physically, usually both! Entertainers, take heed, when you are trying to communicate with an Organizer, be prepared to hear more detail than is absolutely necessary. When you give them information, be prepared to prove anything you present as fact, because Organizers take nothing at face value.

Relaters want warmth, caring and genuine concern expressed in communication to them. They want you to take a slow, gentle approach. They are bowled over by the displays of forcefulness that so impress the Commander. They prefer a more laid-back approach. They want to know how much you care before they will care how much you know.

However, Relaters aren't likely to get a whole lot of warmth and gentle flowing conversation from the average Commander. Commanders consider schmoozing a terrible waste of their time. Why waste time trying to soothe sensitive folks when there's a world to conquer? Nonetheless, Commanders, if you want to communicate with a Relater effectively, you will need to use a soft, unhurried approach so as not to bowl them over, frighten or intimidate them.

Entertainers love color and flair. They can talk endlessly, but aren't especially adept at listening. They love big, broad, sweeping statements and detest a lot of details. Because they don't usually listen well, it's especially important to be sure you have their attention when you're talking to Entertainers. If you don't, don't be surprised if you ask them to do something and it doesn't get done. And then when you ask them why they didn't do it, don't be surprised if they insist you didn't ask. If they aren't listening, they aren't hearing. Entertainers like a lot of social chat mixed in with the serious stuff. In fact, they would just as soon skip the serious stuff, unless you can give it some color and an element of excitement.

Organizers find all the pizzazz tiring, and the Entertainers' penchant for jumping from subject to subject very unsettling. Organizers want everything presented in a precise order. Organizers often just throw up their hands and walk away from an over-enthusiastic Entertainer, convinced that the Entertainer is beyond communicating with. Face it Organizers, if you want to communicate with an Entertainer effectively, you'll have to learn to use lots of color and pizzazz, and keep the details to a minimum, please.

By learning to communicate with others *their way,* you'll get the results you want more readily, and you also will be better able to help others get their results. That can't help but add to your overall happiness and make the shared parts of your life's journey far more wonderful.

Recommended Reading:

• *Conversational Magic,* by Les Donaldson

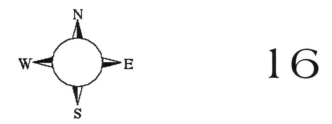

Clearing the Way

We've built some valuable bridges, and now it's time to clear the way to your ideal lifepath. We do that by clearing away some of the old, useless beliefs, habits and values, erroneous self-perceptions, and other forms of garbage we have been lugging around.

We created some of our negative beliefs and habits ourselves, after we became adults. Relatively speaking, these are the easy part to clear away. We can usually change old habits and beliefs formed in adulthood much easier than we can change the long held ones formed when we were children. That's because we can more easily see the reasons for creating the habit or belief we formed as adults, and can weigh those reasons against the reasons for changing them.

For instance, if you started smoking as an adult, just to have something to do when you were at a club, giving it up once you saw it was detrimental to your health would be much easier than if you had started smoking as an adolescent to look cool and adult-like. That's because the reason you started smoking as an adult isn't as powerful as the reason for quitting. But how about looking cool and adult-like? Every adult wants that! So, it comes down to either being healthy, uncool and childish-looking, or taking a health risk in order to remain cool and adult-like.

We don't know this consciously, of course, and that's the problem. We bought into most of our childhood programs for reasons other than the obvious. Most of them were "purchased" from someone else before we were old enough to reason things out. Our parents gave us some of them, when we were growing up, in their attempts to protect us and teach us how to be responsible citizens. Their intentions were usually good, but sometimes their methods were lacking. What's worse, we took everything presented to us in a life or death context, because we didn't know any better.

We got messages that affected our view of ourselves from other places too (teachers, siblings, playmates, bosses, spouses, friends and myriad other people). Some of the input was positive and helpful and some was negative and detrimental to our development. Some of the messages may have been intentionally negative (guilt, fear, force and manipulation) but most of them were probably intended to encourage us to learn or conform in some way.

It doesn't really matter where all the negative stuff came from or what the intention of the giver was, the outcome was the same. We still arrived at adulthood lost, confused and not too sure of what we should be doing now that we have the freedom to do it. The problem now isn't what happened in the past, it's what we have chosen to do with it.

Some of us think that the only way we can rid ourselves of the negative, or at least lighten our burden, is to dump our garbage on others. But dumping on others only makes matters worse because people are active and reactive by nature, and when someone unloads their garbage on us, we tend to toss it right back, adding in some of our own in the process. Relationships can get pretty messy as we continue tossing ever larger piles of garbage on one another.

This craziness stops only when we realize that we are *not* our garbage, and neither is anyone else. We must learn to look past the negative programs, erroneous beliefs, unrealistic expectations, anger, accusations, and all the other nasty stuff we carry around and project onto other people. Just as importantly, we have to learn to look past all of the above in others too. It's the only way to let go of the judgments and harsh criticisms that keep us feuding, fighting and hiding from one another. And it's the only way we can let go of past perceptions that have hurt and limited us. Until we turn loose of the old, we cannot grasp the new.

Until we decide that we have the right, as adults, to leave the old beaten path and discover a new and better one, we will remain stuck in past limitations. We are surely more capable of creating effective selves now than we were when we were three or four years old, which is when many of the old programs were created.

By now you should have a pretty good grasp of what you need to make the desired changes. You have spent a lot of time examining both your nature and your nurture, identifying your personal boundaries and building a stronger foundation. You have the basic tools to begin bagging up the old garbage and clearing it from your path. You also have the basic information to begin charting your own course and defining your own ideal lifestyle. Once you define your ideal lifestyle and decide to live it, free of criticisms and harsh judgments, and free of all the old garbage, you will discover exquisite levels of freedom and peace of mind. Nothing you will ever do will give you as much happiness and contentment as will letting go of harsh judgments. This includes judgments and criticisms of yourself, as well as of others, in both the giving and the receiving of them. You can't imagine how much improved your life and all of your relationships can be until you've taken this important step.

An amazing thing happens when we start to rid ourselves of judging, criticizing, and other negative programs and belief systems. We begin to see how useless these behaviors are, and realize we don't really want or need the burden. Then we can begin purposefully eliminating all the negative stuff from our lives. Soon we discover the old negative aspects are diminishing. We aren't weighing ourselves down with a lot of garbage anymore, neither are we heaping it on other people. It feels great! Then we realize that we don't feel compelled to take other people's garbage anymore, so we refuse to accept it when they try to toss it our way. We just politely hand it back to them and go about our own business, unruffled and unencumbered. That feels great, too!

At this point you might be thinking this all sounds good, but isn't that easy! You're right. It isn't easy, but it can be done. I've done it and so have many others. The outcome is worth every moment you give it and every effort you will make. This step is crucial to your overall happiness and you will definitely want to take it.

Action Step: Clearing Away the Debris

In this step you will examine your thinking processes, your attitudes and your belief systems to uncover and eliminate those that have been detrimental, and to enhance those that are beneficial. You probably

discovered when you did your childhood memories
exercise that many of the old, core beliefs are hard to
uncover. We adopted our core beliefs when we were very
young and we seldom, if ever, question them. Sometimes,
we are completely unaware of them, yet they are controlling us in very powerful ways.

Core beliefs can be beneficial. (I should be kind and
loving, honest and forthright. I am smart and capable. I can
do anything anyone else can do, if I set my mind to it.) Or
they can trip us up and cause us to doubt, and even dislike,
ourselves. (I am so clumsy. I can't do anything right. I
always say the dumbest things. I am not capable of
succeeding. I should be ashamed.). The possibilities are
endless, and the results are often devastating. Unfortunately,
we tend to focus on the negative things, and either discount
or take for granted the positive. We assume the things we
see in ourselves (good or bad) are what we are, and we think
we are stuck with them, whether we like them or not. Know
right now that this is not the case.

The reason you *think* you own the things you don't
like about yourself is because you assumed other people's
estimations of you were accurate long before you were
capable of determining for yourself who you really were or
what you were like.

1.   List outside your personal boundary circle all the
     negative things you have believed about yourself or
     remember hearing others say. Realize that the image
     you hold of yourself may be inaccurate.

2.   Examine the things you have listed outside your
     personal boundaries circle. Compare them to the
     things you have inside your circle. Realize that the
     things outside the circle are all false perceptions that
     someone sold you on while you were still an innocent

little child. Now let yourself feel mad or sad or whatever you need to feel. Feel the injustice of having all this garbage heaped on the innocent, helpless child you were. Feel the anger and the anguish of your inner child as it realizes that it's been duped!

Don't be too concerned about uncomfortable feelings at this point. People often feel constrained and uncomfortable in the midst of a transition, much like a caterpillar must feel while confined to a tight, dark, brittle cocoon after being accustomed to crawling around rather freely. But, when we have worked our way through the discomfort, what we experience at the other end is nothing short of a miracle. It feels just like the emerging butterfly looks — light, joyous and free! Free to explore new heights and to experience life from a broader, more beautiful perspective.

3. Now console the child. Tell it everything will be all right. Tell it you will take care of it and will never let anyone hurt it again. Feel the child's reaction. If it is wary or untrusting, continue to reassure it until you feel it has accepted that you will take care of it. You will know it has accepted the adult you when you experience its joy!

We really begin to break free of our own constraints when we start to question the validity of the old belief systems. We have spent most of our lives looking for evidence that will validate our negative beliefs about ourselves and, unfortunately in the seeking, we typically find plenty. Often, by the time we reach adulthood, negative beliefs are so encrusted by "evidence" that there is simply no doubt in our minds that they are valid.

A good example of how we manage to validate beliefs that are not necessarily true is superstitions. Let's look at an earlier example of believing that it's "bad luck" for a black cat to cross your path. Suppose on your way to work one day, a black cat crosses in front of you. You just "know" that bad luck is now on its way. For the next ten days, however, you have a streak of really good luck and things are going really great! Then, on the eleventh day, something bad happens. Aha! There it is! You knew it was going to happen. It had to. The black cat crossed your path. Now you have forgotten the ten days of glorious good luck and you are focusing on the one bad incident. That's because that one incident is what validates your belief. You validate false beliefs about yourself in exactly the same manner.

4.   Begin to look for and list every fact you can find that will *invalidate* all the old beliefs, all the negative things that lie outside the circle you created to represent your personal boundaries. If, for example, you listed, "I'm not good with people," look at the entire picture. There are bound to be people in the world that you relate to and are "good" with. How about a family member? A friend? A co-worker? A store clerk? A child? Whatever you find that invalidates the *completeness* of the negative statement, write it down.

As you might imagine, eliminating old beliefs that we have spent a lifetime "validating" won't be especially easy, even when we can clearly see that the old beliefs aren't serving our purposes. It can be done, however, so keep at it.

5. Begin to consciously and consistently work at changing your old self-perceptions by monitoring and replacing the self-talk around which any negative sub-personalities have formed (the Critical Parent, the Shamed Child or any other you uncovered).

6. You have most likely heard and read a great deal about positive affirmations and visualization techniques, and perhaps, like me, you have tried several methods with varying degrees of success. If you're still at it, keep it up. I would only suggest that you *personalize* the affirmations you use to suit yourself. Sometimes the ready-made ones won't suit your needs and you won't get the result you want. State affirmations in first person, present tense. "I am...." *not* "I will be...." "I am" tells the subconscious mind that *now* is the time to begin. "I will be" puts the action in the *future,* where it stays! Look at the positive attributes inside your circle and begin stating "I am" affirmations connected to these ... "I am a great communicator." "I am good at problem solving." "I am a kind, loving parent." "I am confident and sure of myself," and so on.

    Don't be surprised if the affirmations or self-corrections which are contrary to the old belief systems feel uncomfortable when you first begin using them. Sometimes affirmations and corrections can feel like *outright lies* initially.

    When an affirmation is interpreted by the subconscious mind as a lie, you will notice that you have a physiological response to the statement, just as though you had actually told a lie. You may feel guilt, or fear, or some other uncomfortable emotion, as well. Don't let these dissuade you. Continue to repeat them to yourself. Tape them on your bathroom mirror. Stick them on the face of your computer. Write them in your daily planner. Do whatever it takes to keep reminding yourself of the positive messages. Your initial resistance will diminish as you continue substituting positive statements for the negative ones.

At some point in the future, you'll realize that when you make the positive statement, you no longer get a negative response. At that point it's time for a personal celebration, because what that means is that your subconscious mind has bought into the new, positive statement and has rewritten the internal program and effectively incorporated it into your everyday life.

What's really wonderful about that is that when the subconscious buys into a new statement and incorporates it, you then *own* the statement as a new belief system. From that point forward, the subconscious mind works just as hard to validate and keep the new belief as it did to validate and keep the old one. There will be no strain, no struggle and no need to use any form of willpower to maintain it. At the point that your subconscious mind buys into the new statement, a paradigm shift occurs and the new, positive program is now as automatic and effortless as the beating of your heart.

7. Try the direct approach.
  A. Get into a relaxed state to move your mind to the Alpha state of consciousness. This is that reverie state that you experience as you are falling asleep at night or first thing in the morning just as you are

waking up. It is that state where you are aware of everything around you, but your body is so relaxed that you don't really want to move. You can induce that state at any time by learning how to relax your body and focus your mind, such as can be achieved in meditation. Or you can take advantage of the fact that you are already entering that state twice a day (first thing in the morning and last thing at night).

B. Once in the Alpha state, begin monitoring your self-talk and/or your thinking processes, and replace the old, negative messages with more positive ones. Be sure that the new messages are rational and believable to you because, if they aren't, your subconscious mind will reject them. "I'm the best!" shuts the subconscious mind down just as fast as "I can't do anything right!" The first statement creates a shutdown because it is not believable. It's too subjective. How can we possibly believe we are "the best" when we are unaware of the capabilities of the millions of other people on Earth? The latter statement shuts us down because it says we can do nothing right, so why try? The key is to find other, more believable alternatives that you can buy.

C. Continue this process on a regular basis until the subconscious accepts the new option as valid. And, to boost the effect, you might want to use the "as if" process in conjunction with the self-monitoring. Here you act "as if" the desired thing were already a reality.

For example, if you tend to always be late, begin to act as if you were timely. As you can see, acting *as if* you are timely would require you to *be* timely. Acting as if you were confident would not necessarily require you to be confident in the beginning, but the subconscious tends to learn quickly through experiential processes. Going through the motions will bring about the desired result much quicker.

This may sound too simplistic, and you may resist the idea that you can change your life by changing your thinking. I understand. I used to think the same thing. Positive thinking has been carried to such an extreme over the years that we tend to dismiss it as just so much New Age mumbo-jumbo. We can't prevent bad things from happening in our lives by thinking positively. We can't necessarily affect what happens in the outside world. What positive thinking *can* change is our thinking processes, our internal representations of ourselves and of the world we live in.

We don't keep the office bully from being his usual nasty self by thinking positively, but we do improve our response to the bully. We don't avoid conflict or irritations, but we do handle them better. Put away any resistance you may be feeling, because the surest way to clear the garbage out of your life is by clearing up your thinking. Everything you believe you are begins right there inside your mind. The old adage, "You are what you think you are," is very true. Your thoughts control your emotions, your emotions control your actions, and your actions control your outcomes. So to keep your emotions and outcomes under control, you must control and guide your thinking.

The power of your mind will pave the way, get you moving and keep you forging ahead. It is the power of your spirit, however, that will guide you gently along the way, and keep you walking your path with integrity and honesty. It is the power of spirit that will move you beyond mere satisfaction and lead you to contentment and real joy. Which brings us to our final leg of the journey.

Recommended Reading:

- *Core Transformations,* by Connirae Andreas
- *Heart of the Mind,* by Connirae Andreas and Steve Andreas
- *How to Have Confidence and Power with People,* by Les Giblin
- *Mastering Your Moods,* by Dr. Melvin Kinder
- *People Skills,* by Robert Bolton, Ph.D.

The Home Stretch

"They are advancing in life, whose heart is getting softer, whose blood warmer, whose brain quicker, whose spirit is entering into Living Peace. Those who have this are the true lords or kings of the earth ... they, and only they."

John Ruskin

We are not just bodies, nor minds, nor bundles of feelings. We are all of these and more. We are also the "I" that owns the body, observes the mind and feels the feelings. We are both observer and the observed. The part of us that observes the self and strives to bring it to contentment and joy is what we have come to call spirit.

Every great transformation involves the whole person or it will not, indeed cannot, be complete. To address the whole person, we must address body, mind, emotions and spirit. Ideally, all four of these quadrants are in balance, but that is rarely the case.

Dr. Elizabeth Kübler-Ross, the great teacher and physician who has dedicated her life to easing the burdens of the terminally ill, author of *On Death and Dying* and *Answers on Death and Dying,* observed that everyone is whole, but not everyone is balanced. According to Dr. Kübler-Ross, when one or more of the elements of the body-mind-emotions-spirit quadrant is missing or diminished, the others will expand to fill the gap. We have only so much life energy to expend at any given time, and if we use a disproportionate amount of that energy in one or two quadrants, the energy to do so must be taken from the remaining quadrants. Those quadrants, from which energy is drained, are diminished in expression, because they lack vital energy.

For example, people who ignore their spiritual and emotional quadrants and focus only on the physical and mental ones, allow the physical and mental parts of their lives to grow out of proportion, while the spiritual and emotional parts shrink accordingly. An individual imbalanced in this manner would be overly concerned about his or her looks, about being (or appearing to be) wealthy, about trying (or appearing) to be smart or shrewd, they might over-indulge in physical pleasures, such as food, alcohol, drugs, sex or just about anything else you might imagine that would fall into the physical and/or mental realm. Workaholics, as well as alcoholics, fall into this category.

The Physical Quadrant

The physical quadrant is concerned with appearances. People who are overly invested in the physical quadrant become narcissistic, always preening themselves. They are overly concerned about how they look and about how their lives look to others. They are overly impressed by material possessions and will go into deep debt to put on the "right" show. They are impressed or repulsed by what others have or lack, as well as by how they or others look. To those who place too much emphasis in this quadrant, appearances are everything.

The Mental Quadrant

The mental quadrant is concerned with thinking, gathering knowledge, and understanding the rational, logical world. Those who are overly invested in this quadrant spend most of their time and energy pursuing knowledge and information. They pride themselves in their store of knowledge and look down on those who are less academic. They often come across as stuffy, opinionated, and intolerant of other people's thoughts and opinions. Only the knowledge that is already accepted as fact among the academics has any value, as far as they are concerned. Anyone holding new or "unproven" ideas or opinions are suspect, and are looked down upon. They are often irritated or frustrated by the "ignorance" and "stupidity" of others.

The Emotional Quadrant

The emotional quadrant is concerned with feelings, responses, and the receiving of impressions. One who is imbalanced toward the emotional will be easily hurt, frustrated or angered. They relate to the world and to other people by the way things and people make them feel. Of course, their own feelings are often changing, and their interactions with the outside world change accordingly.

They often feel either helpless and put upon by others, or irritated at the "indifference" of others. Some cry a lot, while others blow up and yell too much. But, however they approach it, life is lived in extreme ways. People with an imbalance toward the emotional can be elated one minute and completely depressed the next; delighted one minute and furious the next. No one can be sure where they stand with this person, because they are never sure themselves. These people tend to find themselves in difficult situations far more than most people, because emotions run pretty much on automatic, and the rational mind is kept on stand-by, under-developed and under-utilized.

The standby, reactionary mode dominates those who are ruled by their emotions. They go through life just reacting. They feel out of control most of the time, because most of the time, they are out of control, and their outcomes reflect it.

The Spiritual Quadrant

The spiritual quadrant is concerned with things like altruistic love, genuine caring, compassion, kindness, wisdom, and all the things that exist beyond the physical, mental or emotional realms. This quadrant addresses our grandest aspirations and our deepest needs. It is the part of us that leads us to thoughts and actions that seem to be greater than we are. It is the part of us that enables us to connect ourselves to a grander scheme and answer questions that would otherwise be unanswerable.

An imbalance toward the spiritual realm often manifests itself in the form of religious zealots who try to push their beliefs off on everyone else and who refuse to accept those who hold different beliefs. This type tends to expend a great deal of time and energy walking a self-imposed chalk line and trying to make others walk it with them. An imbalance in the spiritual quadrant can also be seen in ascetics, who hide themselves away from the world and spend all their time in prayer and meditation, seldom if ever interacting with other people. Neither of these types do much to increase the understanding and acceptance of what spirituality is really all about.

It isn't hard to recognize where the imbalances lie in those who are overly concerned with one or two of the four quadrants. Large imbalances are generally detrimental to the individual and to everyone who has the misfortune of having to deal with such people. Narcissists, who have eyes only for themselves, have an obvious physical imbalance. Stuffed-shirt academics are obvious examples of a mental imbalance. Hand-wringing worriers, constant fretters, and angry exploders are all readily recognizable examples of those with emotional imbalances. The religious zealots, who sometimes kill and maim others in the name of God, are examples of a spiritual imbalance.

Fortunately, most people don't have greatly exaggerated imbalances, but even minor ones can cause difficulties. They can cause us to be overly concerned about the thoughts and opinions of others, or overly worried about our value if we don't have the best credentials, or too emotional to deal with other people effectively, or too judgmental or withdrawn. So, as you grow and continue to improve yourself, try to balance all four quadrants. You'll be delighted with the overall effect.

Physical Health and Balance

In the physical (bodily) quadrant, learn to eat wisely and exercise. Your health is key to your enjoyment of life

and it is definitely not an area to gamble with. There is
nothing sadder than seeing an individual whose mind is
still sharp and who would still love to be taking an active
part in life, but who is unable to do so because of poor
health.

Learn what you need to do to maintain your health,
and then *do* it! That is the best insurance policy there is and
the best predictor of happiness in old age.

We seem to be inundated with information about diet
and exercise these days, so finding good reading materials
on the subject should be no problem. If you feel you lack
sufficient knowledge and need further study in this area, do
yourself a favor and get the information you need.

The latest research suggests that there is more to our
overall physical health than just exercising and eating right.
This research strongly suggests that how we think and
believe directly affects our health and well-being. It seems
to validate the age-old assumption that if the mind and spirit
are healthy, the emotional self and the physical body tend to
follow suit.

Dr. Deepak Chopra, in his book entitled *Growing
Younger,* suggests that the mind and spirit are such powerful
influencers over the body that even the aging process can be
delayed or reversed through proper thinking, beliefs and
behaviors. Specific mental attitudes, personality traits and
positive belief systems have been shown to lend themselves
to strong, healthy bodies well into old age.

Mental Health and Balance

Mental health and balance is crucial to functioning
fully and effectively as a human being. Yet it is the area
most people spend the least amount of time developing. Too

many people believe that their thinking and emotions, which are both crucial to mental health, cannot be managed to any great extent, so they don't bother to try. But to achieve a true balance in your life, and to move purposefully toward a goal, it is important that you take whatever steps necessary to manage your thinking and develop your mind. This requires far more than just pondering your thoughts. Benjamin Franklin said, "You can't plow a field by turning it over in your mind." Neither can you gain the level of knowledge and wisdom you need by just thinking about them.

If, in moving toward your goals and ideals, you discover you need more formal education, get it! Colleges and universities are full of adult learners today. You don't need to become a full-time student to move steadily toward your goals. You can take just one class a year and, while it may take some time to complete your studies, you will still be moving in the right direction.

Don't discount the value of self-education either. Libraries are a source of infinite knowledge, and many great people throughout history were self-educated. Abraham Lincoln, Andrew Carnegie and Thomas Edison were all essentially self-educated men, as were most women prior to the time higher learning was available to them.

Academic intelligence isn't the only form of intelligence, either. The development of any skill that requires thought helps to develop the mental function. Mechanical and technical acuity are examples of forms of wisdom that fall outside the academic, as are keen relationship skills. Relationship skills are actually more dependent on emotional intelligence than on mental intelligence, but emotional intelligence proceeds from mental awareness.

Emotional Health and Balance

In his book, *Emotional Intelligence,* Daniel Goleman lists five areas, or "domains" for emotional "intelligence." These were adapted from the research of psychologists Sternberg and Salovey, who began studying emotions and applying them to a broader view of intelligence. The list is a very good outline of what emotional health (or intelligence) encompasses. The five requirements for emotional health are:

1. *Self-awareness of one's emotions.* This is the ability to recognize a feeling as it occurs. It is the ability to monitor feelings from moment to moment, in order to control them, rather than allowing them to control us.
2. *Self-management of emotions.* This is the capacity to refrain from emotional outbursts, soothe one's own feelings, shake off irritability, gloom or depression, and to bounce back quickly from emotional setbacks.
3. *Self-motivation.* This is the directing of emotions in the service of achieving goals, and paying attention to those things that are important to our overall success. It is a form of self-mastery that allows us to delay gratification and control impulsiveness in order to achieve a beneficial long term result.
4. *Empathy.* People who are empathetic are more attuned to the emotional responses, wants and needs of others. They are attuned to the social signals that indicate a need for compassion, concern or action on their part, for the benefit of another.

5.   *Handling relationships effectively.* This is an art
      form in the emotional arena. Managing your own
      emotions as well as the emotions of those you
      interact with is the crux of social competence. This
      ability is the foundation of popularity, leadership
      and interpersonal effectiveness.

Spiritual Health and Balance

What constitutes spiritual health seems on the surface
to be a very subjective matter, but in reality it is as much a
science as are the physical, mental and emotional aspects of
mankind, and as such, can be as easily examined.

Spirituality is that part of us which is perceivable only
in the very depths of our being. It is the eternal truth that
exists somewhere within the content of all knowledge and
understanding; truth that can't necessarily be measured and
quantified or even fully expressed, only deeply felt and
understood.

The essence we call "spirit" is beyond the physical
self and the mental self, although it can profoundly affect
these parts of us. Spirit is a gentle guide and comforter to
the emotional self, which enables us to believe in possibilities that extend far beyond our own perceived abilities.
Most of us see our own possibilities as quite limited, but we
perceive God or Spirit as unlimited. Placing our faith in the
unlimited expands our potentials and leads us to things far
greater than we might dare imagine without such faith.

Spirit is that part of us that has been most instrumental
in the creation of every good thing that man has ever
accomplished or learned under any name. But it goes
several steps further than mere learning has ever managed
to take us. That which we call "spirit" somehow reaches

beyond the intellect and touches something deeper inside us; something called love, something called purpose, something called joy, peace, tranquility; something called hope.

Though I didn't recognize it in those early years, it was that element of hope that gave me something to cling to when everything else seemed so elusive. Hope of someday understanding. Hope of finding truth. Hope of improving myself and my circumstances. Hope that the answers existed somewhere, if only I could find them. Hope that I *would* find them. It was this element of hope that caused me to turn back to the spiritual aspect of self, which I had abandoned years earlier and, in the process, I discovered a whole new dimension to "spirituality."

Your spiritual self is a very integral part of who and what you are. If you have turned away from that part of your being in the past or resisted exploring it, it may be because spirit has been presented to you in a less than appealing manner. Perhaps you had it drilled into you as a child that looking at the spiritual aspect of yourself meant feeling shame and guilt for being and acting like a human being. Perhaps you decided it felt better to just ignore that part of yourself than to deal with all the fear and dread you associated with it. Perhaps you preferred not to think about the perceived punishment that you were led to believe was the end result of being less than perfect.

If you grew up in a Western culture, perhaps you learned that to be Christian meant that you were born a "sinner," whose only hope of salvation was sacrifice and submission to some ancient, and often narrow, rules. Perhaps you were taught that certain everyday pleasures were "sinful" and you would "go to Hell" if you indulged in them.

If any of this applies to your current thinking, it would be to your advantage to consider a different picture of your spiritual self. Then you can decide for yourself what is right and true. Discovering your true spiritual nature (which is very gentle, loving, non-judgmental, accepting and kind) will enable you to embrace your own spirituality confidently and with great joy.

I have discovered in my work with hundreds of people, and in my own inner explorations, that at the core of every single human being resides a very pure and beautiful spirit self, quietly waiting to be discovered. This perfect inner-being has great wisdom and it knows exactly what you need to be perfectly whole and happy. It is working every moment of every day for your benefit, and once you recognize it's there, you can tap into that great power and reap all the marvelous benefits it has to impart to you. Tapping this spiritual core can propel you toward health, happiness and wonderful relationships faster than anything you could possibly imagine.

Like most Americans, I was raised in a traditional Western religion, which I found to be narrow, stifling and more harmful to my psyche than helpful. But, as my self-awareness grew, I realized that the spiritual aspect was not just necessary, but actually *core* to my being, so I began a personal search into this realm. In doing so, I discovered there was far more to spirit than most Western religions would have us believe, and certainly more than many of the modern day sciences teach. I highly recommend that you conduct your own search, free of any dogma or religious constraints, and draw your own conclusions, based on what you discover.

My own stubborn refusal to accept anything on blind faith is what initially led me to begin searching on my own.

My search led me to anything and everything that I could find on religion and philosophy, both Western and Eastern, as well as psychology, biology, physiology, and anything else that could add to my body of knowledge and help me to discern truth. Much of the information I gathered outside of mainstream Western religions painted a completely different picture of God than the one to whom I had been exposed. Instead of a fearsome, vengeful, punitive God who threw "sinners" into eternal Hell, these other, more gentle sources painted a picture of a kind, ever-loving, ever-forgiving God; a God who was completely just and who didn't inflict pain and punishment for "sins."

Some of the philosophies I studied described a perfectly neutral, and yet beneficial Creative Force which manifests in a totally benign way. This description of the Creative Force matches more closely the view of some of the scientific communities, which see "God" as a creative force that is evolving to higher and more complex levels.

In many non-Western or non-traditional religions and philosophies, "sins" are described as errors, and errors can always be corrected. There is no such thing as "unforgivable sins," only paths that lead you toward the Creator, or keep you flowing in harmony with the Creative Force, or paths that lead you away from it. Those that lead away also lead to pain and misery, not because you are being "punished" by some vengeful God, but because pain and misery is a *natural* consequence of going the wrong way or doing the wrong thing. Spiritual laws work exactly the same way physical laws do.

If, for example, you touch a hot stove, the experience causes you pain; not to "punish" you, but to let you know that you need to remove your hand from that particular situation. Any pain we experience at a spiritual level is simply a result of doing something that violates a natural spiritual law, just as the hand on the stove violates a natural physical law. The difference is that when we make errors or do something stupid at a physical level, like putting our hand back on the stove even when we know it will burn us, we tend to place the blame for the resultant pain where it belongs; on ourselves and our own foolish actions.

We don't blame "God" when we continue to press on the accelerator of a car, rather than hitting the brake, and crash headlong into the side of a mountain. We realize that we did something wrong, made a mistake, violated some very natural law, and must now suffer the consequences of those actions. We don't blame the mountain for being there, or the car for having an accelerator. That would be ridiculous! Yet many Western fundamentalist religions look at the very natural consequences we experience when we violate natural and beneficial spiritual laws, as "the work of the devil" or "the wrath of God." And far too many Westerners have been subjected to that kind of thinking.

Most other religious and/or spiritual sources, such as Buddhism, Hinduism, Yoga, Taoism, Transpersonal Psychology and Metaphysics view the consequences of violating spiritual laws as being just as natural and predictable as are the consequences of violating physical laws.

Looking at life's events as natural occurrences, rather than as "punishment" increases our understanding and acceptance of spiritual laws and, once we understand and accept them as good and natural, we can learn to avoid the consequences of violating them, just as we do with the physical laws we now understand.

Years of study and direct experience leads me to believe that the gentler teachings and philosophies empower us rather than take our power away. They are not only truer to our spiritual nature, but are far more beneficial to our daily living. I am convinced that these gentler, more beneficial teachings (which include the actual teachings of Jesus, by the way) are the ones we should be modeling for a healthier overall perspective. A view of spirituality as a gentle discipline leads to right action, inner-peace, harmony, thoughtfulness, non-judgment, love and acceptance. Surely these are more spiritual attributes than are guilt, fear, intolerance and condemnation.

An Overview of the Spirit Nature

When matters of the spirit are viewed from a more genuine and realistic position, it is easy to see how and why certain teachings have endured throughout time. For example, ancient master teachers taught that we should not judge and condemn one another because to do so would bring difficulties upon ourselves. This same truth is being taught today in both spiritual and psychological disciplines.

From a psychological standpoint, when we judge and condemn others, we do so in order to avoid looking at those same attributes in *ourselves*. Disowned attributes tend to grow and become more difficult because we are projecting them outward rather than working to improve, eliminate or understand them. Also, by projecting them onto others, we tend to focus on them more, and we usually expand and develop what we focus on. What we expand and develop becomes more dominant in our lives and, if that happens to be some negative attribute which we refuse to deal with, we keep finding ourselves right in the middle of the very things we would prefer to eliminate from our lives.

A good example of expanding and developing a negative attribute to one's own detriment is a man I had in one of my assertiveness workshops. Bill said he was there because he wanted to learn to be less aggressive. He kept getting fired from jobs and wanted to learn how to deal with people more effectively in order to eliminate that problem. I asked him why he thought he kept getting fired, and he answered that it was because he kept ending up working around and for "a bunch of idiots." He stated that he believed that ninety-seven percent of the people in the world were "ignorant" and he just couldn't tolerate ignorance. It was his inability to deal with ignorance, he stated, that usually got him fired.

In Bill's case, he was so focused on the "ignorance" of others that he was unable to see anything else. The fact is, every person on this planet has some area of ignorance. No one knows everything there is to know and, in the areas where knowledge is lacking, we are *all* ignorant. On the other hand, we all have *knowledge* of something, too, and Bill could have just as easily chosen to look for areas of knowledge rather than areas of ignorance in others. Had he done so, his opinion of people would have been very different and so would his outcomes. He was creating his own problems, and intensifying them, by being judgmental.

I suggested to Bill that he spend the week between workshop segments trying to find areas of *intelligence* in others, rather than areas of ignorance, and report his findings at the next session. He returned the next week beaming! He told the class that one bit of advice had made the entire workshop worth his while. I talked to Bill several months later. He was working at a sales job, which he said would have been impossible for him with his earlier attitude and focus. He reported that his change of focus, and subsequent change of belief, had improved his whole life — not just his work, but his relationships and general sense of well-being, as well.

This is just one example of how things we have been taught through religious disciplines apply to everyday life in some very practical, non-mystical ways. Actually, a great deal of what has been taught for centuries through religions is being taught today in the name of psychology. The major difference is that psychology seeks to eliminate all the mysticism and present these truths in more rational, thinking ways. Yet the mystical seems to add to our well-being just as much as any other aspect of ourselves. We need the spiritual dimension, no matter what we choose to label it, as well as the logical to feel content, whole and truly happy.

It is the spiritual aspect of ourselves that enables us to expand our love, compassion and kindnesses beyond our immediate selves and families, and to reach out to assist and embrace others, including complete strangers at times. Spirit is the stuff that great societies, as well as great people, are made of.

I find it fascinating that at the basis of all true forms of spiritual teachings are the same tried and true formulas as are used today in the modern sciences. Centuries-old spiritual teachings tell us that we should love and respect ourselves and our fellow beings equal to ourselves. Today that is a part of developing self-esteem and effective human interactions.

The ancients taught that we should practice patience, tolerance and helpfulness toward one another. The value of this lesson has been shown again and again through modern psychological, as well as interpersonal, disciplines. We do ourselves great damage, both mentally and physically, when we allow impatience and intolerance to keep us upset and off-balance. Mental disorders, depression, anxiety, bleeding ulcers, migraine headaches, heart attacks and high blood pressure, to name just a few, are the by-products of these negative emotions (not to mention poor relationships and personal miseries). According to recent research, a person's level of intolerance is a better predictor of heart trouble than is diet or lifestyle. That's how powerful and detrimental to a person's well-being negative attitudes and beliefs can be.

Many of the sciences such as medicine, psychology and biology which usually take either neutral positions on spirituality or deny it altogether, are ironically adding to the understanding of these truths in greater and greater measure. Science is enabling us to take the truth of spiritual laws out of the realm of mysticism and blind faith and understand them as naturally occurring and beneficial laws, which work side-by-side with the more obvious physical laws, and which are absolutely necessary for our world to exist with any semblance of order.

For example, many medical doctors have acknowledged the power of faith to heal, where all else has failed. Dr. Margaret Cadillo of Harvard Medical School, in her research on how relaxation facilitates healing, discovered that people who tapped into the peacefulness of what they called "spiritual awareness" had an "increased closeness to a power or energy that enhances their well-being." The reason for this, according to her colleague, Dr. Herbert Benson, author of *The Relaxation Response* and *The Wellness Book: The Comprehensive Guide to Maintaining Health and Treating Stress-Related Illness,* is that, when we are under stress, our bodies release hormones and chemicals that increase our metabolism, heart rate, blood pressure, breathing rate and muscle tension. These combined responses eventually lead to all kinds of physical distress, which leads to mental distress and which, all too often, results in very poor outcomes materially.

Achieving the state of balance that allows for deep relaxation and the proper regulation of the bodily systems, requires that we trust in something. It is that element of trust or faith that falls into the spiritual realm. Sufficient levels of faith have been shown to ease pain, eliminate illnesses, end depressions, cure cancers, lower blood pressure, and do a whole lot of other measurable and even miraculous things. These have been tested and documented, not by religious leaders, but by doctors and research scientists.

That spiritual laws and truths can be explained, in part, in modern terms and according to modern interpretations in no way diminishes them. Quite the contrary. It proves their validity. That the ancient masters from around the world knew what today's sciences are just now proving to be true is, I think, remarkable. It is sufficient for me to be willing to examine and apply, through pure faith for the moment, the elements of possibility which spiritual disciplines propose, but which are as yet a mystery to our modern scientists.

Actually, spirituality and science are not nearly as far apart as some people seem to think. Both are searching for the truth of our being, and perhaps the joining of these two important disciplines will occur at some point in the future to the great benefit of us all. Until that time occurs, however, it would be to your benefit to seek truth from every discipline and discover for yourself the greatness and the wonders of life as a whole. Keep your mind open to everything. Assume the responsibility for proving or disproving everything to your own satisfaction, so that you move through life with an internal knowing, rather than with blind faith. You will discover that the pursuit of life and wisdom from a broad and accepting perspective will amply reward you in every area of your life.

In your search to find what is good and true, what is truly genuine and beautiful about yourself and the world in which you live, choose to look not only at the physical, mental and emotional aspects of yourself and others, but at the spiritual aspects as well. Learn to toss out guilt and "sin" and see instead, correctable error. Knowing that errors are correctable, and that the discomforts we feel when we are in "error mode" are simply indicators that corrections are in order, is a truly liberating thing. It's wonderful to realize that by simply correcting errors we can eliminate those vague and persistent discomforts we have been feeling.

The Bible describes this as "repenting" (correcting errors) so that your "sins" (errors) can be "forgiven." When we "forgive," as in forgiving a debt, we forget it. So to "forgive sins" would be to let go of, or forget, past errors and focus on moving in a more positive and beneficial direction. That makes perfect sense when viewed without all the mysticism, doesn't it?

A classic example of this is a teenage boy named Travis. Travis felt angry and resentful toward his parents, who he said were "trying to control his life." To "punish" them, and to feel victorious over them, he began to drink, take drugs and stay out all hours of the night. This, of course, caused the parents to tighten the reins, which caused Travis to fight and resist all the more. After years of such counter-productive behaviors, Travis' parents finally gave up, realizing that they had no real control over him, and that he would just have to live with the consequences of his actions.

Travis went wild for awhile, got into trouble with the law and ended up in jail. His parents didn't go to his rescue. They had informed him, when they gave up trying to help him, that he would have to bear the consequences of his actions, and they were as good as their word. Thirty days in jail gave Travis time to rethink his actions and where his life was headed, and he decided, of his own accord, that he was destroying his own future.

When he got out of jail, Travis stopped the drinking and drugs, stopped running with the wild bunch he had taken to, and began to take his schooling more seriously. Today Travis is a junior at a very good college, and is an honor student. He is studying developmental psychology. His goal is to work with parents and teenagers to help them co-exist more harmoniously, and to help teenagers find their own path and aim for it early in life.

Both Travis and his parents were violating a spiritual law, "sinning," by trying to force their wills on one another. Never in history have forced behaviors been met with positive reactions. Religion sees the "law of non-resistance" being violated here. Science sees it as "friction" between two opposing views. Psychology sees it as "conflict." But, no matter how it's viewed or what it's called, the results are the same. And the only way to stop having the negative results is to change the behavior of your own accord or "repent," as Travis did.

Positive, long-term changes are always a result of realizing that we are responsible for our own outcomes, and then taking the necessary steps to move forward in more positive directions. As we let go of past mistakes and learn to use them as guideposts to prevent our making the same mistakes in the future, we in effect "repent." Eventually, this self-correcting system leads us to our own ideal place in life and we discover happiness, contentment and a self that turns out to be quite lovable, warts and all.

When we are able to love ourselves and fully accept our own "flaws" as easily as we accept our strengths and positive attributes, we are also able to develop the capacity to love and accept others more fully. When we are fully accepting of self and others, we are able to give up anger, resentment, judgments, criticism, and all the other negative, separating thoughts and behaviors that go with these attitudes. In place of all those negative, uncomfortable emotions and attitudes that have plagued us in the past, we find happiness, peace, contentment, joy and greater understanding of ourselves, other people, and of the world as a whole.

The wonderful truths that lie at the basis of the disciplines we call "religious" or "spiritual" have persisted over the ages because they point us toward the very core of our beings, and it is within that core that we discover true peace, happiness and well-being. Whether we label these disciplines religion, psychology, philosophy, science or whatever is irrelevant. What is relevant is that they work. They always have and they always will, because as humans we will always have the same basic needs. Those basic needs are (and always have been) best filled through love, acceptance, appreciation, kindness, forgiveness, patience, caring, and all the other attributes that are inherent to the *spirit* of humankind.

Those who fail to develop the spiritual portion of themselves, do themselves a great disservice. When that very vital element is missing, we are like eight-cylinder vehicles running on only four cylinders. We lack vitality and personal strength. We lack the cohesiveness that holds all the other elements together and gives us a sense of

purpose. Humans need a sense of purpose, and the greater
the purpose, the better we function.

Explore the things of spirit. Learn for yourself how
the parts all fit together and complement one another when
approached with personal knowledge and understanding.
Develop a balance between your physical, mental,
emotional and spiritual quadrants, and discover what a joy
a life in balance can be.

Action Step: Creating an Awareness of Your Spiritual Self

1. Sit comfortably, with your eyes closed. Relax your
    body and begin to breathe deeply from the abdomen,
    rather than from the chest. Focus on your breathing
    to slow your thought processes down a little.
    Visualize a pleasant, relaxing scene (a placid lake, a
    beautiful park, the beach, etc.) and imagine yourself
    relaxing in the midst of it. Become a part of the
    peacefulness.

    Spend ten to twenty minutes doing this exercise
    two or three times a week. Expect nothing from it
    but peacefulness and calm. From within the calm,
    relaxed, peacefulness your spiritual awareness will
    grow and so will your ability to cope with everyday
    stress.

2. See yourself, at the core of your being, as pure and
    perfect, gentle and loving, yet powerful. This is the
    essence of spirit and you are spirit at your core. Make
    it a goal to connect with this part of your being.

3. Learn to see "sin" as correctable error, and take
    responsibility for making any corrections you need

to make. As you do, you will rid yourself of any guilt or self-condemnation, and move into a more positive, peaceful state of mind.

4. Realize that, as a human being, you will make mistakes. Mistakes don't mean you are "bad." They just mean you still have some learning to do. Keep learning and growing in the awareness that you are moving steadily toward your ideal self. Be kind to yourself and others in the process.

5. Eliminate the tendency to place the value of other people higher than your own value. Be as generous with yourself as you are with others and vice versa. Assign equal value to everyone and the judging, that can be so detrimental to your peace of mind, cannot remain.

6. Recognize your spiritual self in moments of complete joy. Notice how you feel watching a beautiful sunset, listening to beautiful, soul-stirring music, being held by someone you love deeply — this is the voice of your soul. Learn to seek that voice more often. Grow that part of you. Integrate the awareness of it into your everyday life. Your happiness and contentment will increase many times over.

7. Eliminate the need to always be right and to argue for a position. Realize that arguing gains you nothing but tension and ill feelings, neither of which are conducive to spiritual growth. If you don't feel compelled to be right in every situation, even when others are trying to argue with you, you will maintain a peacefulness and calm that will sustain and strengthen you. When arguing for your position or rightness is no longer an issue, you will discover

your observational abilities also growing, and with greater observation comes true wisdom.

A Buddhist master was once approached by one of his disciples. "Master," the disciple began, "there are those in the world who say that we are born just once, and that when we die we never return to the earth plane. And there are those who say that reincarnation is the reality. I ask you, wise Master, which of these sayings is true?" The master looked at the disciple and in the gentle, but authoritative voice of one who knows, answered, "It doesn't matter."

Recommended Reading:

- *The Sound of Soul's Awareness,* by Sherry Buffington
- *The Self-Healing Personality,* by Dr. Howard S. Friedman
- *The Immune Power Personality,* by Henry Dreher
- *Timeless Healing,* by Herbert Benson, M.D.
- *A Return to Love,* by Marianne Williamson
- *Peace, Love and Healing,* by Bernie Siegel, M.D.

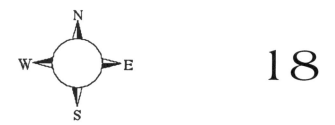

There Is No Final Chapter

We've come a long way together and covered a lot of ground, but your journey is just beginning. And what a glorious journey it will be! You have learned a lot about yourself, and now you are stronger and more prepared to travel your own ideal path. You may still have some work to do, but even that can be enjoyable. Self-discovery is great fun when you know that your "self" is exactly what you want it to be — and it is!

The things you have learned in the pages of this book are by no means all you need to know. My purpose was to get you started in the right direction and to give you some important tools. Your studies will not end here, nor should they. Life is a process of learning that never really ends. The dynamics of life and your part in it will shift from moment to moment, and change as you change and grow. That's what makes life fun and exciting.

You can manage the changes and the pace of your life to suit your needs, but life will continue to unfold before you. Continual observation and learning on your part will ensure that you change and grow in the appropriate ways as life presents itself to you, and the world around you shifts and changes.

As you develop yourself into all that you are capable of becoming, it is important to address the whole of yourself, because if any part of you is left untended it will suffer. And, if any part of you suffers, the whole suffers. Remember: there are four aspects that make up the whole of your being — the physical, the mental, the emotional and the spiritual. When any one of these is left untended, we remain out of balance and off course.

I meet people regularly who have worked for years to develop themselves, but who are still struggling because they have neglected some aspect of their being. When the neglected part is the physical, poor health, obesity, and bad habits like smoking, drinking or not exercising get out of hand and the physical body suffers. When the mental is neglected, the individual fails to learn the things that will propel them forward and upward. It can be something as simple as refusing to correct and improve one's vocabulary, preferring to continue to look ignorant, rather than work on correcting a few misused words. When someone knows what to do to improve one's self, but refuses to do it, that is the height of ignorance. Someone who takes such a position is actually willing to remain wrong in order to feel like he is right! Usually, the only person he manages to fool is himself.

Those who fail to develop at the emotional level tend to be childish, selfish, thoughtless or inconsiderate of others. They are too needy or too temperamental. Life's changes trip them up, frustrate them, and cause them to go into a tailspin, spiraling ever downward. They can't seem to get a grip on their lives or their outcomes, and they let life's adverse moments confound them rather than help them learn new coping skills. They often feel helpless to find their own solutions and call their own shots.

Those who fail to develop at the spiritual level may have wealth, power and position, but they still feel something important is missing. That's because the part of themselves that gives the other three aspects meaning and cohesion has not been developed. What they are missing is joy, peacefulness, contentment, self-love and a full self-awareness. They are missing their connectedness to other people and to life as a whole.

Take the time to develop every aspect of yourself to the highest level possible for you. You will know you have achieved the highest level when you are completely and almost continually happy and content. As you might imagine, this is not a one-shot process. It is an ongoing lifetime journey, so enjoy it. If you keep moving in the direction of your ideal, someday you will find your path starting to smooth out, and the rest of the journey will be delightful, even with all its challenges!

I have made that transition myself, and I have seen many others make it, too, often in a much shorter time than I did. Many of my students have told me that their transformation time was shortened because I had helped them assemble the necessary tools into one place, so they could begin to use them more effectively. That has been my goal here as well. To shorten your search and improve your response time, I have endeavored to give you, in this book and in the recommended reading lists, the basic tools you need to effect your own transformation.

If you have done the exercises along the way as recommended, and if you have expanded your studies in the areas where you felt you needed additional information, you have arrived at this point much more self-aware, and with a far better understanding of yourself. You have some idea as to what your ideal lifestyle looks like, and a better awareness of the path you want to be walking. You know the importance of self-monitoring, of being fully responsible for your outcomes, and of building good relationships with those who will accompany you through life. You realize that *you* are, and have been, the primary source of your problems and you know that *you* are the solution, as well. You know your strengths, and are building on them. You are aware of your weaknesses, and you have developed some strategies to help you to compensate for, or overcome, these.

You have some tools for learning to deal with fears and insecurities more effectively. You understand how your nurturing has affected your nature and you know which old programs you need to eliminate from your psyche in order to allow your nature to emerge in the most beneficial way.

You now have some new strategies to help you feel more in control of your own life, and as you begin to walk your own life path, you will walk it with greater confidence, because it is *your* path, and no one is better equipped to walk it than you are. You know what additional tools you will need for your continued growth and you know, at least in part, where to find these additional tools.

There is one more thing I would like to give you before we part — a conscious awareness of that all important, life-directing instrument — your compass. Who's got the compass? You have it! You've had it all along, right there inside you. Your compass is one of a kind, and it is exclusively yours. No one else has a compass that can guide you more truly or more surely than your own. It guides you by responding with feelings of joy, pleasure, delight, contentment, peacefulness and other positive responses when you're on track, and with feelings of friction, discomfort, irritation, anger, pain, misery and other negative responses when you're off.

You can learn to read your compass correctly by getting and staying in touch with your inner self. Once you are fully aware of the very clear signals your body, mind, emotions and spirit are constantly broadcasting to you, and once you start using those signals correctly, you'll never get lost again. You may get off track occasionally, but when you do, you'll know it almost immediately, and you will be able to quickly correct your course and continue confidently on your journey. Your compass will always let you know, through your feelings, what "off track" and "on track" feels like, if you are paying attention.

Learn to notice negative feelings and to keep altering your course until positive feelings tell you you're back on track. In time, you will gain a true appreciation of your compass' capabilities and you will learn to trust it completely. Let it guide you along your pathway safely and surely. Pay attention to its subtle, but undeniable cues. They can lead you to the mastery of your life's journey.

If you've taken all the steps and done all the work throughout this book, you've invested a lot of time and energy, and you've invested it wisely. Your investment will serve you well.

If you have not finished the exercises, please go back and complete them. Make it a point to find any additional information you may need to continue progressing. If you think you want to improve your life, but aren't willing to take the necessary steps to do so, you are simply fooling yourself. You can't make substantial changes in your life by simply reading and dreaming. It is *vitally important* that you determine what you want to accomplish, set goals, develop the plans to reach those goals and then, *take action.* Do the steps! You're worth the effort.

Look ahead now to the road that stretches out before you, begging to be explored. Approach it as a willing adventurer who is ready to accept almost any challenge. There will always be challenges. They are a part of life. But, having come this far, I know you are an explorer who can handle them.

As you continue along this road we call life, understand that the road does not change. It doesn't suddenly become smoother or less challenging. But the road isn't ours to change and we need not concern ourselves with that. How we meet life's challenges is what makes all the difference. Challenges stretch us and make us stronger, more capable human beings, so welcome them, learn from them, and then move beyond them.

Though we can't change the road, the people we meet along the road, or the events of life as they unfold before us, we have *complete* power to change one very important thing — *ourselves.* When we have done that successfully, everything else seems to fall into place somehow. Life seems to flow along more peacefully and we flow right along with it. All the little irritations, and even the bigger trials and tribulations, become a part of the process and we learn to remain calm and at peace even in the midst of these.

At that point we don't need to try to change the road. We don't need to try to change other people. We begin to see everything simply as a part of life's experience and we learn to let the experience teach us in beneficial ways.

In Robert Frost's poem, "The Road Not Taken," he wrote, "I came to a wood where two roads converged and I … I took the one less traveled by, and that has made all the difference." Frost's "less traveled road" was his own unique path. Your path is also the one less traveled. It is yours and yours alone and when you step onto it, you will realize that it does make all the difference in the world.

We have traveled together as far as we can for now. It's time for you to head off in the direction of your own ideal. But, having made it this far, there's no question you have what it takes to succeed at the ultimate quest — that of self-mastery, and the claiming life's greatest treasure — a self-directed life. A wonderful, lifelong adventure awaits you now, you've earned it, so go for it!... and enjoy the journey!

For information on workshops, retreats, books or tapes available through Peak Potentials, or to obtain a copy of the complete C.O.R.E. Multi-dimensional Awareness Profile write to:

Peak Potentials

8730 King George Drive
Dallas, TX 75235
Phone: (214) 688-1412
E-mail: sdb@coremap.com
Visit our web site at www.coremap.com